D1635039

You think you're clever...
but are you the *Brainiest*?

If you are up for the challenge, why not try
Britain's Brainiest Family Quiz Game?

- Over 2,200 questions
- At retailers nationwide

©2002 Celador International Limited

BRITAIN'S BRAINIEST

B☘XTREE

First published 2002 by Boxtree
an imprint of Pan Macmillan Ltd
Pan Macmillan, 20 New Wharf Road, London N1 9RR
Basingstoke and Oxford
Associated companies throughout the world
www.panmacmillan.com

ISBN 0 7522 15094

Produced under license from Celador International Limited

© 2002 Celador International Limited

The Britain's Brainiest logo is the property of Celador Productions Ltd

The rights of Celador to be identified as the author of this
work has been asserted by them in accordance with the
Copyright, Designs and Patents Act 1988.

All rights reserved. No part of this publication may be
reproduced, stored in or introduced into a retrieval system, or
transmitted, in any form, or by any means (electronic, mechanical,
photocopying, recording or otherwise) without the prior written
permission of the publisher. Any person who does any unauthorized
act in relation to this publication may be liable to criminal
prosecution and civil claims for damages.

1 3 5 7 9 8 6 4 2

A CIP catalogue record for this book is
available from the British Library.

Designed and typeset by seagulls
Printed and bound by Mackays of Chatham plc

CONTENTS

Your challenge is to become the *Brainiest*! Work your way through the first 2 rounds, plus the bonus Missing Links and Code Breakers, gaining as many points as possible to ensure your place in the final round.

ROUND 1
1-6 players
You have 5 seconds to answer each multiple choice, general knowledge question. Enter your scores on your score sheet (starting on page 249). Each correct answer is worth 1 point.

MISSING LINKS
1-6 players

Example

Quiz _____ Shop

This Missing Link is BOOK : Quiz <u>Book</u> Shop

This is your chance to score extra points. You have 90 seconds to find the Missing Link to as many of the 4 shown as possible. Enter your scores on your score sheet. Each correct answer is worth 1 point.

CODE BREAKERS
1-6 players

Example

| 1 | 3 | 2 | 6 | 6 | 0 |
Type Of Fruit

This Code Breaker is Cherry 1 = C, 3 = H, 2 = E, 6 = R, 6 = R, 0 = Y

Each digit represents a letter from the keypad. For example, the digit 1 in a Code Breaker could represent an A, B or C, the digit 2 could represent a D, E or F and so on.

This is another chance to score extra points. You have 90 seconds to crack the Code to as many of the 3 shown as possible. Enter your scores on your score sheet. Each correct answer is worth 1 point.

ROUND 2
1-3 players
In turn, with the highest scorer going first, choose a category from the 6 available and turn to the relevant page. You now have 90 seconds to answer as many of the 12 category questions as you can. Each correct answer is worth 1 point. Once a category has been played it cannot be selected again. Now repeat the process once more so that every player has selected and answered questions from two categories each. Enter your scores on your score sheet. Each correct answer is worth 1 point.

4-6 players
In turn, with the highest scorer going first, choose a category from the 6 available and turn to the relevant page as stated. You now have 90 seconds to answer as many of the 12 category questions as you can. Enter your scores on your score sheet. Each correct answer is worth 1 point.

MISSING LINKS
1-6 players
As before

CODE BREAKERS
1-6 players
As before

FINAL ROUND
1-3 players
The top 3 scorers now play the final round. It's about observation, skill and tactics. There can only be one *Brainiest*!

If you are playing alone, select and answer all your 5 questions BEFORE checking your answers.

Your previous scores are not carried forward in this round and all players begin at 0.

To become the *Brainiest*, your objective is to have the highest score after every player has chosen and played 5 questions each.

The highest score possible in this final round is 15. (e.g. correctly answering 5 opponents specialist category questions).

General knowledge	1 point
Own specialist category	2 points
Opponents specialist category	3 points

The highest scorer from the previous rounds chooses a specialist category from the 8 available and turns the page to find the pre-determined specialist categories for the second and third players.

In turn, with the highest scorer going first, each player can ask for a question from their own category or one from their opponents to earn points and out-tactic each other. If you don't want to answer your category questions you can steal one of your opponents questions and if answered correctly earn more points, or play safe and select a general knowledge question.

But remember, there are only five questions per category so select carefully. Once all 5 questions have been played in a specialist category you may be forced to answer questions from another category or general knowledge questions for less points. You MUST answer 5 questions each.

Enter your scores for each round of questions into your score sheet, keeping an eye on your opponents' scores. After every player has answered 5 questions each, the player with the highest score is the *Brainiest*!

GAME 1

GAME 1

1

Which Republican presidential candidate lost the 1960 US election to John F Kennedy?

| Dwight Eisenhower | 1 | 2 | Richard Nixon |
| Lyndon Johnson | 3 | 4 | Harry Truman |

2

Which is the third planet from the Sun?

| Earth | 1 | 2 | Venus |
| Mercury | 3 | 4 | Mars |

3

Chickpeas are the main ingredient in which popular dip?

| Tsatziki | 1 | 2 | Taramasalata |
| Mayonnaise | 3 | 4 | Hummus |

4

Flamenco is the traditional dance of the Gypsies of which part of Europe?

| Southern Spain | 1 | 2 | Eastern Turkey |
| Northern Ireland | 3 | 4 | Western Italy |

Answers on page 234

5

Complete the title of this children's book by A A Milne, 'Now We Are...?'

Awake ⟨ 1 | 2 ⟩ Six
Quiet ⟨ 3 | 4 ⟩ Young

6

What was the Viennese composer Schubert's first name?

Pieter ⟨ 1 | 2 ⟩ Gustav
August ⟨ 3 | 4 ⟩ Franz

7

Perth is the capital of which Australian state?

New South Wales ⟨ 1 | 2 ⟩ Western Australia
Victoria ⟨ 3 | 4 ⟩ Queensland

8

In which part of the human body would you find the stirrup, the hammer and the anvil?

Eye ⟨ 1 | 2 ⟩ Leg
Ear ⟨ 3 | 4 ⟩ Foot

Answers on page 234

GAME 1

9

With whom did Kylie Minogue duet on the 1988 chart-topper 'Especially for You'?

Stefan Dennis ⟨ 1	2 ⟩ Jason Donovan
Craig McLaughlan ⟨ 3	4 ⟩ Nick Cave

10

On which London square is the National Gallery situated?

Parliament Square ⟨ 1	2 ⟩ Trafalgar Square
Grosvenor Square ⟨ 3	4 ⟩ Sloane Square

11

What is the name of the Duke and Duchess of York's second child?

Eugenie ⟨ 1	2 ⟩ Beatrice
Zara ⟨ 3	4 ⟩ Peter

12

In which film does Bruce Willis attempt to save the Earth from a giant asteroid?

Deep Impact ⟨ 1	2 ⟩ Armageddon
Total Recall ⟨ 3	4 ⟩ Twelve Monkeys

Answers on page 234

Fruit _____ Bowl

Flower _____ Hole

Blue _____ Cake

Solar _____ Game

Answers on page 235

1	3	3	1	2	5

London Landmark

7	5	5

Unit Of Weight

1	1	4	3

Indonesian Island

Answers on page 236

SELECT A CATEGORY

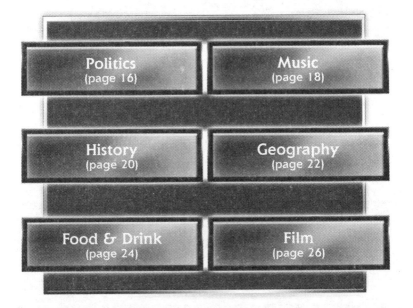

Politics
(page 16)

Music
(page 18)

History
(page 20)

Geography
(page 22)

Food & Drink
(page 24)

Film
(page 26)

GAME 1

POLITICS

1

Who was president of Russia
immediately before Vladimir Putin?

2

The Tynwald Court is the
parliament of which island?

3

In which city is the Scottish Parliament based?

4

What is the maximum number of elected
terms of office a US president can serve?

5

Who was emperor of Japan during WWII?

6

The Taoiseach (pronounced 'tee-shuck')
is the prime minster of which country?

Answers on page 237

POLITICS

7

Gerry Adams is president of
which political party?

8

How long is the term of office of a US Senator?

9

Leopoldo Galtieri was president
of which country from 1981-1982?

10

Which Russian leader was
born Vladimir Ilyich Ulyanov?

11

Ramsey MacDonald was the first prime minister
to come from which of the main political parties?

12

Which Amendment to the US Constitution states that no
person should be compelled to testify against themself?

Answers on page 237

GAME 1

MUSIC

1

Who is the lead singer with Roxy Music?

2

What sort of fish appears in the title
of a famous Schubert quintet of 1819?

3

What is the three-letter name of the band whose
members are Michael Stipe, Mike Mills and Peter Buck?

4

To which city was Glenn Miller flying
when his plane disappeared?

5

Which group has numbered amongst its members
Phil Collins, Mike Rutherford and Peter Gabriel?

6

According to the title of their 1966 number one,
what colour did the Rolling Stones want to 'Paint It'?

Answers on page 237

MUSIC

7

Which group took the 'Last Train to Clarksville' to number 23 in the charts in 1967?

8

Which legendary rock group's album 'The Wall' was made into a film in 1982?

9

According to the Eurythmics and Aretha Franklin's 1985 hit, who 'Are Doin' It For Themselves'?

10

What did Dire Straits get 'Money For' according to their 1985 chart hit?

11

Morrissey was the lead singer with which famous Indie group of the 1980s?

12

According to the title of their 1979 chart-topper, which day of the week did the Boomtown Rats not like?

Answers on page 237

GAME 1

HISTORY

1

What colour rose represented
the House of Lancaster?

2

Who is the second child of
the Prince and Princess of Wales?

3

How many years are mentioned in the first line
of Abraham Lincoln's Gettysburg Address?

4

Which king led the Scottish forces
at the Battle of Bannockburn?

5

Begun on 17th January 1991, what code-name was
given to the allied attack on Iraq in the Persian Gulf War?

6

Who was the only inmate of
Spandau Prison from 1966 to 1987?

Answers on page 237

HISTORY

7

Which Norwegian scientist famously led an expedition on the Kon-Tiki raft?

8

'Ich dien' is the motto of which member of the Royal Family?

9

Which airship exploded in the USA on 6th May 1937?

10

What was the first name of the English king whose piety earned him the epithet 'The Confessor'?

11

With which country did Germany sign a non-aggression pact on the eve of WWII?

12

In which country is Agincourt, the site of the famous battle of 1415?

Answers on page 237

GAME 1

GEOGRAPHY

1

Which river rises 18 miles north-west of Dijon, and flows into the English Channel at Le Havre?

2

Cape Town is the legislative capital of which country?

3

Annapurna is part of which mountain range?

4

What word, from the Greek meaning 'wandering in search of pasture', is applied to any wandering people?

5

The New York borough of Queens contains two major airports, JFK and which other?

6

Which volcanic peak in Washington State erupted in May 1980?

Answers on page 237

GEOGRAPHY

7

The line of latitude at 23 degrees 27 minutes north is the Tropic of ...?

8

Which is the highest peak in Europe?

9

Truro is in which English county?

10

What sort of institution is the famous Uffizi in Florence?

11

The Matterhorn is part of which mountain range?

12

Which capital city is located on Honshu Island?

Answers on page 237

GAME 1

FOOD & DRINK

1

The saliva of which bird is used in Chinese bird's nest soup?

2

Which popular cooking ingredient has the latin name Allium sativum?

3

Traditionally where would wine bottles be stored?

4

Which rich fruit cake shares its name with a Scottish city?

5

The name of which German spirit means a 'gasp' in literal translation?

6

Which long, thin loaf of bread is regarded by many as a symbol of France?

Answers on page 237

FOOD & DRINK

7

Apart from nutmeg which other spice
is obtained from the nutmeg tree?

8

Which long, slender smoked sausage with a very
soft, fine texture takes its name from a German city?

9

In the UK what name is given to
flour with added baking powder?

10

Which word is used to describe
an extra dry champagne?

11

In Cornwall the word 'figgy' is still used
for which common cake ingredient?

12

A morel is what type of food?

Answers on page 237

GAME 1

FILM

1

Which screen siren starred as
Sugar Kane in 'Some Like It Hot'?

2

In which 1998 Steven Spielberg film does Tom
Hanks take a group of soldiers to find Matt Damon?

3

Who plays the title role in the 'Mad Max' films?

4

In which film do Roy Schneider, Richard Dreyfuss
and Robert Shaw fight for survival on a boat?

5

What is the name of the demonic child,
the son of Satan, in 'The Omen'?

6

Which martial arts movie legend co-stars
with Chris Rock in 'Rush Hour'?

Answers on page 237

FILM

7

In which 1963 war film does Steve McQueen play Virgil Hilts, 'The Cooler King'?

8

Which swashbuckling actor stars in the 1938 film 'The Adventures of Robin Hood'?

9

What is the title of the first sequel to 'Alien'?

10

In which 1940 Disney film does Mickey Mouse appear as the Sorcerer's Apprentice?

11

The subtitle of the film 'Star Trek III' is 'The Search for...' who?

12

Which pop megastar made her big screen debut in the 2001 film 'Crossroads'?

Answers on page 237

Pilot _____ Aircraft

Railway _____ Dance

Hair _____ Joint

Roller _____ Board

Answers on page 242

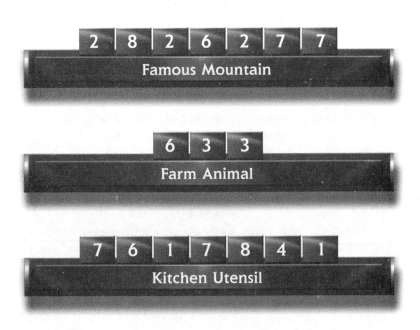

| 2 | 8 | 2 | 6 | 2 | 7 | 7 |

Famous Mountain

| 6 | 3 | 3 |

Farm Animal

| 7 | 6 | 1 | 7 | 8 | 4 | 1 |

Kitchen Utensil

Answers on page 243

WELL DONE SO FAR!

Now each player must add up their individual scores from
each round to get their total score. The highest score possible
is 38. Only the top three scorers can play the final round.

If you scored
0-20

So you think you're the *Brainiest*? Hmmm, maybe a little
revision wouldn't go amiss. Better luck in the next game!

If you scored
21–30

Not bad, not bad at all...but you will have to do
better than that to be the *Brainiest*!

If you scored
31 +

Wow! Top of the class. May see you in the final round!

Now for the ultimate challenge for the top three scorers.
Turn to page 185 and find out if you really are
the *Brainiest* of them all!

GAME 2

GAME 2

1

Wiener schnitzel consists of breaded cutlets of which meat?

Veal	1	2	Pork
Beef	3	4	Turkey

2

Over what distance is the Olympic steeplechase run?

15,000 metres	1	2	1,000 metres
3,000 metres	3	4	9,000 metres

3

What sort of animal is a hoopoe?

Fish	1	2	Bird
Snake	3	4	Insect

4

Which Stephen King novel involves a writer being kidnapped by his number one fan?

Misery	1	2	Cujo
Salem's Lot	3	4	The Dead Zone

Answers on page 234

GAME 2

5

Guantánamo Bay is an inlet on which island?

| Bermuda | 1 | 2 | Cuba |
| Jamaica | 3 | 4 | Antigua |

6

Who rose to fame playing Violet Elizabeth Bott in the 1970s children's show 'Just William'?

| Jane Horrocks | 1 | 2 | Lena Zavaroni |
| Bonnie Langford | 3 | 4 | Emma Thompson |

7

Which painter, who reputedly sold only one painting during his lifetime, had an art dealer brother called Theo?

| Gustave Courbet | 1 | 2 | Camille Pissarro |
| Edgar Degas | 3 | 4 | Vincent Van Gogh |

8

In which film do the characters Mr Pink, Mr White, Mr Orange and Mr Blond appear?

| Pulp Fiction | 1 | 2 | Reservoir Dogs |
| Desperado | 3 | 4 | From Dusk Till Dawn |

Answers on page 234

GAME 2

9

The Seychelles is a group of islands in which ocean?

Arctic	1	2	Atlantic
Pacific	3	4	Indian

10

Which football club has been managed by Ron Atkinson, Stuart Pearce and Brian Clough?

Fulham	1	2	Sheffield United
Tranmere Rovers	3	4	Nottingham Forest

11

Who directed the 2001 remake of the film 'Planet of the Apes'?

George Lucas	1	2	Michael Mann
Tim Burton	3	4	Steven Spielberg

12

Which plant has the botanical name Narcissus?

Thistle	1	2	Daffodil
Rose	3	4	Shamrock

Answers on page 234

Ticket _____ Junior

Jelly _____ Fingers

Green _____ Boat

Car _____ Camp

Answers on page 235

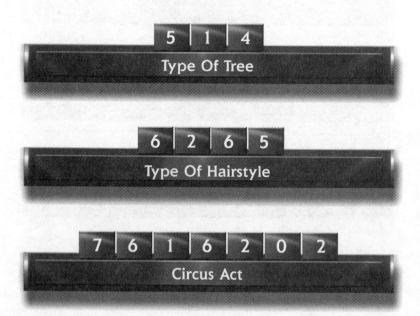

| 5 | 1 | 4 |

Type Of Tree

| 6 | 2 | 6 | 5 |

Type Of Hairstyle

| 7 | 6 | 1 | 6 | 2 | 0 | 2 |

Circus Act

Answers on page 236

SELECT A CATEGORY

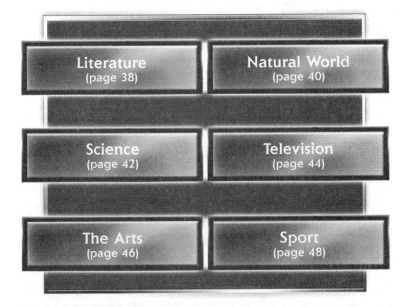

Literature
(page 38)

Natural World
(page 40)

Science
(page 42)

Television
(page 44)

The Arts
(page 46)

Sport
(page 48)

LITERATURE

1

Which character created by Dorothy L Sayers has become one of the great fictional detectives?

2

Who is missing: Happy, Sleepy, Doc, Bashful, Sneezy, Grumpy and ...?

3

Which poet and novelist wrote a series of 'Barrack-Room Ballads' in the early 1890s?

4

In literature what Greek word means the power to arouse feelings of pity or sorrow?

5

Which Scottish poet wrote the words for 'Auld Lang Syne'?

6

Who wrote the original short story 'The Reluctant Dragon' which became a Disney film in 1941?

Answers on page 237

LITERATURE

7

What is the name of the two-headed animal in the Doctor Dolittle books by Hugh Lofting?

8

The form of prose known as the saga originated on which island country?

9

What sort of creature is Curious George in the books by H A Rey?

10

'Blott on the Landscape' published in 1975 was a success for which British author?

11

Which stately home was 'revisited' by Charles Ryder in Evelyn Waugh's 1945 novel?

12

What general name is given to a goddess that inspires a creative artist?

Answers on page 237

GAME 2

NATURAL WORLD

1

How many pairs of legs does a spider have?

2

By what name is the insect-eating plant, Dionaea muscipula, more commonly known?

3

Which is Britain's national bird?

4

To which country is the kiwi native?

5

What type of domestic pet is a Dandie Dinmont?

6

By what name is the male reproductive organ of a flower known?

Answers on page 237

NATURAL WORLD

7

What name is given to the tiny plankton-like crustacea which are eaten by whales?

8

The rowan is another name for which European tree?

9

Which seabird is also known as the 'Bottlenose' or 'Sea Parrot' because of its multicoloured beak?

10

By which other name is the garden plant Impatiens commonly known?

11

Which warm-water fish can inflate its body with air or water as a means of defence?

12

The leaves of which plant are popularly used to relieve nettle stings?

Answers on page 237

GAME 2

SCIENCE

1

Which Polish astronomer first postulated the theory that the Earth moves around the Sun?

2

What does the lachrymal gland produce?

3

Which invention of 1956 became essential to women worldwide as the mini-skirt became the fashion?

4

How many acres are there in a square mile?

5

Which is the main artery in the human body?

6

What name is given to the treatment of foot conditions?

Answers on page 237

SCIENCE

7

Which planet is closest to the Sun?

8

What part of the human body
is affected by astigmatism?

9

Which Adolphe presented his new woodwind
musical instrument at the 1841 Brussels exhibition?

10

How many major planets
are there in our solar system?

11

Which fluid, produced by glands in the mouth, marks
the beginning of digestion in the human body?

12

What device was invented
by Alessandro Volta in 1800?

Answers on page 237

GAME 2

TELEVISION

1

What is the name of the
police station featured in 'The Bill'?

2

Which long-running show created by
Phil Redmond is set in a London school?

3

Who plays TV's Alan Partridge?

4

What is the name of Jill Harvey's
daughter in 'Crossroads'?

5

Which 'Play School' presenter
is the narrator of 'Trumpton'?

6

In which cult series does Number Six
try to escape from The Village?

Answers on page 237

TELEVISION

7

Which soap is set in the sprawling
Scottish estate of Glendarroch?

8

As played by Melissa Joan Hart,
Sabrina is a 'Teenage...' what?

9

Which comedian's nickname is 'The Big Yin'?

10

With what sort of TV shows are Johnny Carson
and David Letterman most associated?

11

What is the name of the yellow creature who accompanies
Ash on his journey in the 'Pokémon' TV series?

12

Which 'Blackadder' star presents the
archaeological show 'Time Team'?

Answers on page 237

GAME 2

THE ARTS

1

Which black actress won the Best Actress Oscar at the 2002 ceremony for her performance in 'Monster's Ball'?

2

Which surrealist artist designed the dream sequence in Hitchcock's film 'Spellbound'?

3

Willy Loman is the central character in which Arthur Miller play?

4

How is the painting 'La Gioconda' better known?

5

Which German word meaning 'trash', is used of garish, pretentious or sentimental art?

6

What is the name of the female dance group that has appeared at Radio City Music Hall since 1932?

Answers on page 237

THE ARTS

7

Who is Shakespeare's 'Moor of Venice'?

8

Which abstract artist was
nicknamed 'Jack The Dripper'?

9

Jean Butler was the dance partner of which
'Riverdance' choreographer and star?

10

Which is the oldest existing
ballet company in England?

11

What are actors urged to 'break' as part
of a traditional theatrical good luck wish?

12

Which ballet features the
'Dance of the Sugar Plum Fairy'?

Answers on page 238

GAME 2

SPORT

1

Which city hosted the 2002 Winter Olympics?

2

What nickname was given to the American Olympic champion Florence Griffith-Joyner?

3

First held in 1930, by what name are the British Empire Games now known?

4

Which British athlete was helped over the finishing line by his father, after tearing a hamstring in the 1992 Olympics?

5

For which type of sporting event is Bisley, in Surrey, a famous venue?

6

Which annual London sporting event was founded by former Olympic steeplechase champion Chris Brasher?

Answers on page 238

SPORT

7

At the 1924 Olympics, why did Eric Liddell
refuse to compete in the 100 metres?

8

In which sport has the Milk Race
been the premier event in Britain?

9

Which US racecourse hosts the
Kentucky Derby every year?

10

For which football league club did the legendary
Tom Finney play throughout his professional career?

11

Which sport holds its British Open Championships
annually at Cowdray Park, West Sussex?

12

In the 1952 Olympics, the legendary athlete Emil Zatopek won gold
medals in the 5,000 metres, 10,000 metres and which other event?

Answers on page 238

Stop _____ Dog

Round _____ Wine

Bullet _____ Reading

Paint _____ Coaster

Answers on page 242

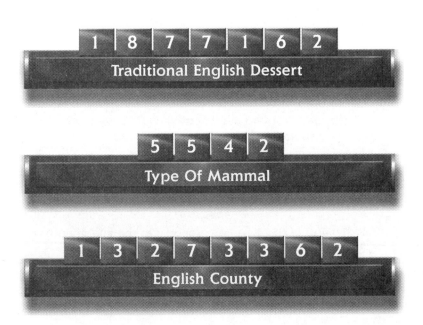

| 1 | 8 | 7 | 7 | 1 | 6 | 2 |

Traditional English Dessert

| 5 | 5 | 4 | 2 |

Type Of Mammal

| 1 | 3 | 2 | 7 | 3 | 3 | 6 | 2 |

English County

Answers on page 243

WELL DONE SO FAR!

Now each player must add up their individual scores from
each round to get their total score. The highest score possible
is 38. Only the top three scorers can play the final round.

If you scored
0-20

So you think you're the *Brainiest*? Hmmm, maybe a little
revision wouldn't go amiss. Better luck in the next game!

If you scored
21-30

Not bad, not bad at all...but you will have to do
better than that to be the *Brainiest*!

If you scored
31+

Wow! Top of the class. May see you in the final round!

Now for the ultimate challenge for the top three scorers.
Turn to page 185 and find out if you really are
the *Brainiest* of them all!

GAME 3

1

What orbits the Earth once every 27.32 days?

The Moon	1	2	Jupiter
The Sun	3	4	Mars

2

The Duma is one of the houses
of which country's parliament?

Germany	1	2	Russia
France	3	4	Italy

3

What sort of weapon was invented
by Richard Gatling in 1862?

Machine gun	1	2	Tank
Land mine	3	4	Hand grenade

4

Who was the original astrologer on the BBC's
'Breakfast Time' when it launched in 1983?

Justin Toper	1	2	Russell Grant
Mystic Meg	3	4	Claire Rayner

Answers on page 234

5

Which artist built a vast garden at his house in Giverny, which he used as a subject in many paintings?

Vincent Van Gogh	1	2	Henri de Toulouse-Lautrec
Claude Monet	3	4	Paul Gauguin

6

Sukiyaki is a popular beef and vegetable dish from which country?

Finland	1	2	China
Russia	3	4	Japan

7

Who was the last Labour prime minister before Tony Blair?

Ramsay Macdonald	1	2	Clement Attlee
James Callaghan	3	4	Harold Wilson

8

Which treaty, signed at the end of World War I, established the League of Nations?

Treaty of Rome	1	2	Treaty of Versailles
Oslo Accords	3	4	Good Friday Agreement

Answers on page 234

9

Where was the singer/songwriter Van Morrison born?

Northern Ireland	1	2	Germany
USA	3	4	Norway

10

Who pioneered the use of antiseptics?

Marie Curie	1	2	Joseph Lister
Ernest Rutherford	3	4	Christiaan Barnard

11

Which part of the body might be affected by lumbago?

Back	1	2	Ear
Hair	3	4	Teeth

12

In computing what does the acronym CAD stand for?

Controlled auto-delivery	1	2	Computer-aided design
Conceptual article dragging	3	4	Complete amplification denied

Answers on page 234

Turtle _____ Brace

Orange _____ Court

Trump _____ Shark

Gold _____ Cake

Answers on page 235

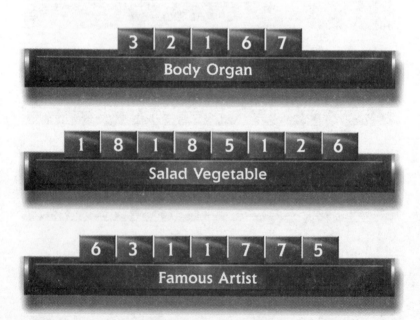

| 3 | 2 | 1 | 6 | 7 |

Body Organ

| 1 | 8 | 1 | 8 | 5 | 1 | 2 | 6 |

Salad Vegetable

| 6 | 3 | 1 | 1 | 7 | 7 | 5 |

Famous Artist

Answers on page 236

SELECT A CATEGORY

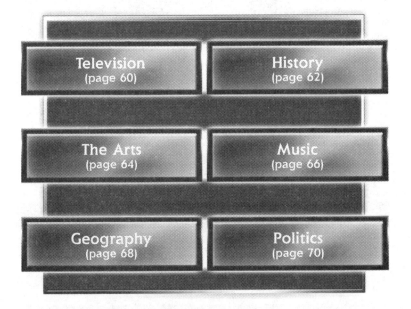

Television
(page 60)

History
(page 62)

The Arts
(page 64)

Music
(page 66)

Geography
(page 68)

Politics
(page 70)

GAME 3

TELEVISION

1

Who plays Albert Steptoe in 'Steptoe and Son'?

2

Which 'Emmerdale' actress
presents 'You've Been Framed'?

3

Complete the title of this children's
cartoon series, 'Butt Ugly...'?

4

Which long-running travel show is
presented by Judith Chalmers?

5

Bella, Milo, Fizz and Jake are collectively
known as which children's TV characters?

6

Which soap is set in Melbourne's
Wentworth Detention Centre?

Answers on page 238

TELEVISION

7

What is Blackadder's first name
in the four main series?

8

Who is Sooty's panda girlfriend?

9

Which 1970s heart-throb plays
Rodney Blackstock in 'Emmerdale'?

10

'Duty Free' is set in a hotel in which country?

11

What was the name of TV's 'Battery Boy'?

12

Which comedian wrote and
appeared in the 'Q' series?

Answers on page 238

HISTORY

1

Ho Chi Minh was president of which country?

2

A title belonging to the British sovereign, what is the meaning of 'Fidei Defensor'?

3

Which British colony was handed back to China in 1999?

4

To which royal house did Richard III belong?

5

What type of bomb was exploded by the USA for the first time at Eniwetok Atoll in the Pacific, in 1952?

6

Which knitted headwear takes its name from a battle in the Crimean War?

Answers on page 238

HISTORY

7

From which country did Iceland
achieve independence in 1944?

8

What name was given to the independent
republic proclaimed in East Pakistan in 1971?

9

The father of which member of the
Royal Family was Prince Andrew of Greece?

10

Who was the Soviet leader at the
time of the Cuban missile crisis?

11

Which ocean liner was sunk by a
German submarine on 7th May 1915?

12

The Battles of Cold Harbor, Bull Run
and Shiloh were all part of which war?

Answers on page 238

THE ARTS

1

What colour is the artist's pigment bitumen?

2

Which art movement was founded
by Pablo Picasso and Georges Braque?

3

Complete the title of this Tennessee
Williams play, 'Cat on a Hot Tin...'?

4

Which ballet company is based at the
Royal Opera House in Covent Garden?

5

Which 19th century French artist, known for his
paintings of Paris nightlife, was only five feet tall?

6

What is the theatrical term for a final rehearsal at which
everything is done as it would be in a real performance?

Answers on page 238

THE ARTS

7

Which artistic 'Brotherhood' was founded by Rossetti, Holman Hunt and Millais?

8

If an actor is said to 'chew up the scenery', what are they doing?

9

Which pop artist was the manager of the rock group The Velvet Underground?

10

Ginger Rogers was whose long-time dancing partner?

11

Which Shakespeare play features the line, 'A horse! A horse! My kingdom for a horse!'?

12

Which English pottery designer is famous for her Bizarre ware?

Answers on page 238

MUSIC

1

What nationality was the composer Jean Sibelius?

2

'Aspects of Love' is a 1980s
musical by which composer?

3

Which Bee Gees chart-topping hit
shares its title with the name of a US state?

4

According to Meat Loaf's 1978 hit,
how many 'Out of Three Ain't Bad'?

5

Which German composer spent most of his life in England
where he composed 'Music for the Royal Fireworks'?

6

What did Cliff Richard combine with 'Mistletoe'
in the title of his 1988 Christmas No 1?

Answers on page 238

MUSIC

7

Squeeze's 1979 top ten hit said it was 'Cool For...' what sort of animals?

8

Benjamin Britten's 'War Requiem' incorporates nine poems by which WWI poet?

9

In 1978 Barbra Streisand and Neil Diamond reached the top ten with 'You Don't Bring Me...' what?

10

Which 'City Limits' were the subject of Ike and Tina Turner's 1973 hit?

11

Stéphane Grappelli was a famous virtuoso on which instrument?

12

The famous theme tune to which series of films starring Peter Sellers, was composed by Henry Mancini?

Answers on page 238

GEOGRAPHY

1

What was the name of South Africa's racial segregation laws which ended in the early 1990s?

2

Of which east African country is Addis Ababa the capital?

3

Which constellation appears on the flags of both Australia and New Zealand?

4

July 4th is celebrated in the USA as the anniversary of the adoption of which document?

5

With which country is the guerilla organisation the Tamil Tigers most associated?

6

Which river runs through the centre of Dublin?

Answers on page 238

GEOGRAPHY

7

The hadj is the pilgrimage every adult Muslim must make to which holy city?

8

By what acronym is the main armed Basque separatist organisation in Spain known?

9

Which river became famous for a gold rush in 1896 after a discovery at Bonanza Creek?

10

The Incas established their capital at Cuzco in which modern-day country?

11

Koblenz lies at the junction of the Mosel and which other river?

12

Which native American chief commanded the Sioux army against Custer at Little Bighorn?

Answers on page 238

GAME 3

POLITICS

1

Media tycoon Silvio Berlusconi became prime minister of which country in 2001?

2

The leader of which of the three main UK political parties stepped down after the 2001 General Election?

3

Who along with Friedrich Engels wrote 'The Communist Manifesto'?

4

Jiang Zemin became president of which country in 1993?

5

In the late 1980s the famous 'Clause 28' prohibited local authorities from promoting what?

6

Who was Bill Clinton's vice-president?

Answers on page 238

POLITICS

7

According to legend which US president, as a boy, couldn't lie about chopping down a cherry tree?

8

Which president of Egypt was assassinated in 1981?

9

Which interviewer famously angered Defence Secretary John Nott in 1982, by calling him a 'Here today, gone tomorrow politician'?

10

Under which US president was George Bush Snr vice-president?

11

What was the name of the political organisation expelled from the Labour Party in 1986?

12

The US Congress comprises the Senate and which other house?

Answers on page 238

Sky _____ Board

Reading _____ House

Poached _____ Shell

Time _____ Meal

Answers on page 242

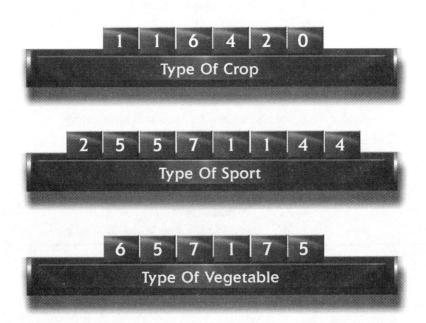

| 1 | 1 | 6 | 4 | 2 | 0 |

Type Of Crop

| 2 | 5 | 5 | 7 | 1 | 1 | 4 | 4 |

Type Of Sport

| 6 | 5 | 7 | 1 | 7 | 5 |

Type Of Vegetable

Answers on page 243

WELL DONE SO FAR!

Now each player must add up their individual scores from
each round to get their total score. The highest score possible
is 38. Only the top three scorers can play the final round.

If you scored
0-20

So you think you're the *Brainiest*? Hmmm, maybe a little
revision wouldn't go amiss. Better luck in the next game!

If you scored
21–30

Not bad, not bad at all...but you will have to do
better than that to be the *Brainiest*!

If you scored
31+

Wow! Top of the class. May see you in the final round!

Now for the ultimate challenge for the top three scorers.
Turn to page 185 and find out if you really are
the *Brainiest* of them all!

GAME 4

GAME 4

1

Swaziland is landlocked between Mozambique and which other country?

| Egypt | 1 | 2 | Libya |
| South Africa | 3 | 4 | Kenya |

2

Which singer was born Steveland Judkins?

| Steve Strange | 1 | 2 | Stevie Wonder |
| Steve Harley | 3 | 4 | Cat Stevens |

3

The leaves of which herb are traditionally used to make pesto?

| Basil | 1 | 2 | Rosemary |
| Dill | 3 | 4 | Parsley |

4

In which year was the Queen Mother born?

| 1907 | 1 | 2 | 1889 |
| 1900 | 3 | 4 | 1898 |

Answers on page 234

5

Who wrote the play 'Waiting for Godot'?

Eugene O'Neill	1	2	Samuel Beckett
Arthur Miller	3	4	Edward Albee

6

Which 1970s sitcom starred
Sid James and Diana Coupland?

Sykes	1	2	Robin's Nest
Bless This House	3	4	Porridge

7

How long is an American Football
field from goal line to goal line?

200 yards	1	2	80 yards
120 yards	3	4	100 yards

8

The Vistula is the longest river in which country?

Germany	1	2	Poland
Turkey	3	4	Iraq

Answers on page 234

GAME 4

9

Who was British prime minister
at the outbreak of World War II?

| Neville Chamberlain | 1 | 2 | Alec Douglas-Home |
| Stanley Baldwin | 3 | 4 | Anthony Eden |

10

Which 'EastEnders' character
is played by Sid Owen?

| Ian Beale | 1 | 2 | Mark Fowler |
| Simon Wicks | 3 | 4 | Ricky Butcher |

11

What is the name of the barrister character who is
the subject of several novels by John Mortimer?

| Horace Rumpole | 1 | 2 | Harry Hotspur |
| Jonathan Wild | 3 | 4 | Charles Endell |

12

The biathlon combines cross-country
skiing with which other discipline?

| Ice skating | 1 | 2 | Rifle shooting |
| Discus throwing | 3 | 4 | Long jump |

Answers on page 234

Wall _____ Pot

Road _____ Bean

Pencil _____ Study

Cable _____ Wash

Answers on page 235

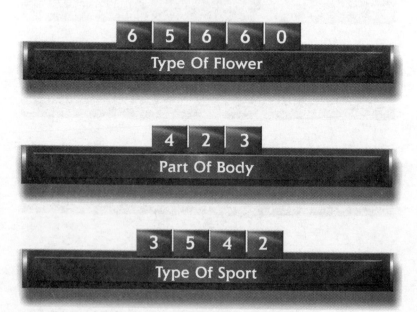

| 6 | 5 | 6 | 6 | 0 |

Type Of Flower

| 4 | 2 | 3 |

Part Of Body

| 3 | 5 | 4 | 2 |

Type Of Sport

Answers on page 236

SELECT A CATEGORY

Food & Drink
(page 82)

Science
(page 84)

Natural World
(page 86)

Film
(page 88)

Sport
(page 90)

Literature
(page 92)

GAME 4

FOOD & DRINK

1

Whose Biblical name is given to a baked pudding, consisting of an upper layer of sponge and a lower layer of apples?

2

From which country does the cheese Emmental originate?

3

Which important source of protein can be cooked 'sunny-side-up'?

4

What type of pastry would traditionally be used to make éclairs?

5

With which Christian festival is Simnel cake most usually associated?

6

If you ordered 'wonton' in a Chinese restaurant what would you receive?

Answers on page 238

FOOD & DRINK

7

Dunlop is a type of which food?

8

Which edible fruits and their relatives are classed botanically under the name Prunus?

9

A cutlet is a chop from which part of a sheep or lamb?

10

Apart from milk what is the other main ingredient of traditional English custard?

11

What name is given to the melted fat from roasted meat which is used for cooking or as a spread?

12

Ladies' fingers is an alternative name for which vegetable?

Answers on page 238

GAME 4

SCIENCE

1

Which 'meal' consisting of a chemical element and water, is given to patients requiring X-rays of the stomach and intestines?

2

An all-time favourite with children, how did the original invention 'Blibber-bubber' became better known?

3

Which muscles contract in order to bend the leg at the knee?

4

What type of simple camera was invented by George Eastman in 1888?

5

Which vital gland is found at the base of the brain?

6

The invention of the aqualung is attributed in part to which famous undersea explorer?

Answers on page 238

SCIENCE

7

Which king constructed the
Royal Greenwich Observatory in 1675?

8

In biology, what is the basic unit of
which all living things are composed?

9

Which theory of the origin of the universe postulates that it
emerged from a state of extreme temperature and density?

10

When the visible part of the moon
is increasing, it is said to be what?

11

Which planet was discovered in 1930 by
American astronomer Clyde Tombaugh?

12

To whom is the invention of the
revolver hand pistol attributed?

Answers on page 238

NATURAL WORLD

1

Which international environmental pressure group was founded in 1971?

2

The gila monster is a species of which creature?

3

Which type of deer is Britain's largest native land mammal?

4

The pipistrelle is the commonest British variety of which type of creature?

5

What name is given to the 'feelers' on the heads of insects?

6

Concorde, Conference and Merton Pride are all varieties of which fruit?

Answers on page 238

NATURAL WORLD

7

Which large shark, named for its habit of floating at the surface, feeds on plankton?

8

Cantaloupe is a variety of which fruiting plant?

9

The fennec is the smallest species of which animal?

10

By what general name is the young of a whale called?

11

Which creatures would you expect to find living in a vespiary?

12

What sort of plant is bladderwrack?

Answers on page 238

FILM

1

What sort of creatures are cloned
in the 1993 film 'Jurassic Park'?

2

In 'Shrek', for what kind of animal
does Eddie Murphy provide the voice?

3

What is the name of the wizard played by Ian
McKellen in the 'Lord of the Rings' trilogy of films?

4

Which comic book hero has been played on screen
by Michael Keaton, Val Kilmer and George Clooney?

5

In which film does Robin Williams' character
invent a green goo that defies gravity?

6

Which 1980 film comedy features
the line, 'Don't call me Shirley'?

Answers on page 239

FILM

7

In which film does Tom Hanks play a little boy who finds himself in a man's body?

8

Who directed the films 'Blue Velvet', 'Eraserhead' and 'The Elephant Man'?

9

Which Hollywood actor stars alongside Whitney Houston in 'The Bodyguard'?

10

In which film does Mel Gibson play Scottish hero William Wallace?

11

Which revolutionary foodstuff is the title of a 1973 sci-fi film starring Charlton Heston?

12

Complete the title of this epic David Lean film, 'The Bridge On The River...'?

Answers on page 239

SPORT

1

Which club won football's
English FA Cup in 2002?

2

In which event did Eddie 'The Eagle' Edwards
become famous in the 1988 Winter Olympics?

3

Which of the English classics is run at Doncaster?

4

England cricketer Ian Botham played for Somerset,
Worcestershire and which other county?

5

What is the surname of the two brothers who played
for England in the 1966 football World Cup final?

6

Which British triple-jumper won Olympic gold
in the men's event in the 2000 Sydney Games?

Answers on page 239

SPORT

7

What was tennis star
Billie Jean King's maiden name?

8

For which country did David Campese
play international rugby union?

9

Which tennis player married Steffi Graf in 2001?

10

Apart from Sebastian Coe, which other former
athletics world record holder became an MP?

11

Which London football club was
originally called Thames Ironworks FC?

12

In which sport was Britain's
David Broome world champion in 1970?

Answers on page 239

LITERATURE

1

Who was Janet's brother in the series of graded readers first produced for small children in 1949?

2

What is the title of the Washington Irving short story about a headless horseman?

3

Which American science fiction author wrote 'Fahrenheit 451' and 'The Martian Chronicles'?

4

If a line of poetry is written in iambic pentameter, it is divided up into five what?

5

What name is given to someone who writes another person's autobiography for them without taking credit?

6

What sort of bird is hung around the neck of the Ancient Mariner in Coleridge's poem?

Answers on page 239

LITERATURE

7

Who 'came in from the cold'
in a 1963 novel by John le Carré?

8

Which bird repeatedly says 'Nevermore' in Edgar
Allan Poe's famous poem of the same name?

9

In 'The Rescuers' by Margery Sharp,
what is the name of the little white mouse?

10

Which English poet, who moved to the USA
in 1939, had the first names Wystan Hugh?

11

Who was appointed Poet Laureate in 1999?

12

Which English novelist born in 1866, is regarded
as one of the great originators of science fiction?

Answers on page 239

GAME 4

Personal _____ Pants

Television _____ Test

Safety _____ Cushion

Hair _____ Price

Answers on page 242

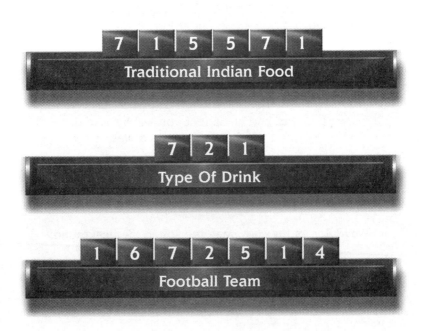

| 7 | 1 | 5 | 5 | 7 | 1 |

Traditional Indian Food

| 7 | 2 | 1 |

Type Of Drink

| 1 | 6 | 7 | 2 | 5 | 1 | 4 |

Football Team

Answers on page 243

WELL DONE SO FAR!

Now each player must add up their individual scores from each round to get their total score. The highest score possible is 38. Only the top three scorers can play the final round.

So you think you're the *Brainiest*? Hmmm, maybe a little revision wouldn't go amiss. Better luck in the next game!

Not bad, not bad at all...but you will have to do better than that to be the *Brainiest*!

Wow! Top of the class. May see you in the final round!

Now for the ultimate challenge for the top three scorers. Turn to page 185 and find out if you really are the *Brainiest* of them all!

GAME 5

GAME 5

1

Complete the title of this 1956 hit for Bill Haley and his Comets, 'See You Later...?'

| Officer | 1 | 2 | Pops |
| My Darling | 3 | 4 | Alligator |

2

Which country has national festivals including Girls' Day, Boys' Day and Golden Week?

| Japan | 1 | 2 | Australia |
| Canada | 3 | 4 | France |

3

The Book of Kells is an important gospel document on display in which city?

| New York | 1 | 2 | Dublin |
| Stuttgart | 3 | 4 | London |

4

Which US sitcom follows the 1950s exploits of the Cunningham family?

| The Brady Bunch | 1 | 2 | Married... With Children |
| I Love Lucy | 3 | 4 | Happy Days |

Answers on page 234

5

Who plays Princess Leia in the 'Star Wars' films?

| Karen Allen | 1 | 2 | Carrie Fisher |
| Kate Capshaw | 3 | 4 | Michelle Pfeiffer |

6

What sort of culinary item is hoisin?

| Sauce | 1 | 2 | Pastry |
| Vegetable | 3 | 4 | Rice |

7

The Battle of Gettysburg was
part of which conflict?

| Boer War | 1 | 2 | World War I |
| American Civil War | 3 | 4 | Crimean War |

8

In South African politics what
do the initials ANC stand for?

| African New Consensus | 1 | 2 | African National Congress |
| Alternative Neutral Chairman | 3 | 4 | Adopted November Charter |

Answers on page 234

9

Which city is the home of the
world's oldest annual marathon?

Paris ⟨ 1	2 ⟩ London
Boston ⟨ 3	4 ⟩ Tokyo

10

What is the name of the ex-SAS commander
who is the author of 'Bravo Two Zero'?

Andy McNab ⟨ 1	2 ⟩ Bernard Cornwell
Tom Clancy ⟨ 3	4 ⟩ James Ellroy

11

In which US state is Graceland,
the home of Elvis Presley?

Texas ⟨ 1	2 ⟩ Michigan
Tennessee ⟨ 3	4 ⟩ Georgia

12

On which continent is Guinea?

Europe ⟨ 1	2 ⟩ Africa
Asia ⟨ 3	4 ⟩ South America

Answers on page 234

Sun _____ Cheese

Trout _____ House

Cat _____ Court

Surf _____ Room

Answers on page 235

| 5 | 7 | 7 | 6 | 3 | 1 | 3 |

Type Of Bird

| 6 | 5 | 4 | 2 | 6 |

Type Of Card Game

| 8 | 5 | 1 | 6 | 2 | 4 | 4 | 1 |

Type Of Rain Shield

Answers on page 236

SELECT A CATEGORY

History
(page 104)

Literature
(page 106)

Science
(page 108)

Food & Drink
(page 110)

Politics
(page 112)

Television
(page 114)

GAME 5

HISTORY

1

In which country did the Battle
of the Boyne take place?

2

Which Turkish seaport and peninsula was the site of a
prolonged battle in 1915 between Turkish and ANZAC forces?

3

Who was king of England at
the time of the Battle of Hastings?

4

Which inlet on the south coast of Cuba was
the site of an unsuccessful invasion in 1961?

5

The Tet Offensive was part of which war?

6

What is the first name of the king of
England who was known as 'The Unready'?

Answers on page 239

HISTORY

7

Which country was at war
with Iran between 1980 and 1988?

8

In 1917 the name of the British Royal Family
was changed from Saxe-Coburg-Gotha to what?

9

Who was commander of the German
forces at the Battle of El Alamein?

10

Prince Edward is the Earl of where?

11

What title did Princess Anne receive
from the Queen in June 1987?

12

The concept of chivalry historically
pertains to which group of people?

Answers on page 239

LITERATURE

1

What is the name of the steam launch in C S Forester's novel about a missionary's sister, and a timid cockney engineer?

2

Which British illustrator is best known for his drawings accompanying the work of A A Milne in the Winnie-the-Pooh stories?

3

How old was Adrian Mole when he began to write his secret diary?

4

Which is L Frank Baum's most famous story?

5

Whose famous 'Waverley' novels were based on the troubled history of the Scottish clans?

6

Which acclaimed novel by Jung Chang tells the painful story of three generations of Chinese women in her own family?

Answers on page 239

LITERATURE

7

In which fictional county
are Thomas Hardy's novels set?

8

Which Russian novelist based his book 'One Day in the Life
of Ivan Denisovich' on his own experience in a labour camp?

9

Who is in charge of the Big Station in
the stories about Thomas, the Tank Engine?

10

Which book by Salman Rushdie, published in 1988,
caused offence to many Muslims around the world?

11

Charlie Bucket is the central character
in which Roald Dahl book?

12

Who wrote the poem 'The Waste Land'?

Answers on page 239

GAME 5

SCIENCE

1

Which rays for examining the inside of the body did Röntgen discover in 1895?

2

A solution of acetic acid found in the kitchen would be more familiarly known as what?

3

Which zoologist wrote 'The Naked Ape' and 'The Human Animal'?

4

What name is given to the point in the celestial sphere directly above the observer?

5

Which device produces the mixture of air and petrol in internal combustion engines?

6

What was the name of George Stephenson's famous steam engine of 1829?

Answers on page 239

SCIENCE

7

Which element has the chemical symbol H?

8

What is the anatomical name for the longest and strongest bone in the human body?

9

Which doctor pioneered the human heart transplant operation in South Africa in 1967?

10

Whose oath has been adopted by the medical profession as an ethical code or ideal?

11

What nationality was Gabriel Daniel Fahrenheit, the physicist who gave his name to a thermometric scale?

12

Which common British tree shares its name with a form of transport?

Answers on page 239

GAME 5

FOOD & DRINK

1

With what is the Greek wine retsina flavoured?

2

Which dish means 'little rice' in Italian?

3

In wine-tasting terminology, what feature of wine is referred to as 'the robe'?

4

Which universally consumed drink is made from the leaves of the shrub Camellia sinensis?

5

What name is given to the scraping of citrus peel used as a flavouring?

6

Which expression of Italian origin, meaning 'all the fruit', is a variety of ice-cream?

Answers on page 239

FOOD & DRINK

7

What is the main ingredient
of a traditional mock turtle soup?

8

Which word is traditionally used
to describe a dry, still white wine?

9

Unleavened bread is lacking
which usual bread ingredient?

10

Which world-famous amber-coloured wine is
named after a little town in north-east Hungary?

11

In Spain, what name is given to the assortment
of hors d'oeuvres served with apéritifs?

12

Slivovitz, a popular brandy in eastern
Europe, is made from which fruit?

Answers on page 239

GAME 5

POLITICS

1

Which Conservative leader launched his 'Back to basics' policy at the 1993 party conference?

2

What shape is the Kremlin?

3

What first name was shared by the 1980s West German chancellors Schmidt and Kohl?

4

Which Conservative Secretary of State for Defence resigned over the Westland affair in 1986?

5

Whom did Thabo Mbeki succeed as president of South Africa in 1999?

6

In which Japanese city was a protocol on climate change signed by 160 countries in 1997?

Answers on page 239

POLITICS

7

Marshal Tito was president of which European country?

8

In 1972 who became the first US president to visit China whilst in office?

9

Who was Britain's longest continuously serving prime minister since 1827?

10

The donkey is the symbol of which US political party?

11

What is the first name of Mrs John Major?

12

By what name is the Red Cross known in Muslim countries?

Answers on page 239

TELEVISION

1

How are the children's TV amphibians Donatello, Leonardo, Michaelangelo and Raphael better known?

2

In 'Coronation Street' who is the father of the baby Maxine gave birth to in 2002?

3

Which cartoon character's catch-phrases include 'Ay Carumba!'?

4

In 'Coronation Street' which proprietor of the Rovers Return was played by Doris Speed?

5

Who became the chairman and presenter of 'Question Time' in 1994?

6

What is the name of Robbie Jackson's dog in EastEnders?

Answers on page 239

TELEVISION

7

In which soap was Trevor Jordache
buried under the patio?

8

Which character does Bill Owen
play in 'Last of the Summer Wine'?

9

In the television standard known
as HDTV, what does 'HD' stand for?

10

Who sings the theme song to 'Dad's Army'?

11

On which part of their bodies
do the Teletubbies have a TV screen?

12

Which sitcom features the oft-repeated line, 'Leesen
verrry carefully, I weel say zees only once...'?

Answers on page 239

Fortune _____ Monster

Window _____ Car

Cost _____ Edge

Mouse _____ Door

Answers on page 242

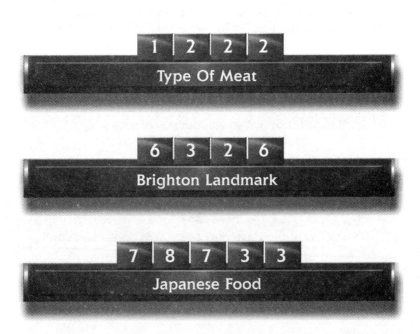

1	2	2	2

Type Of Meat

6	3	2	6

Brighton Landmark

7	8	7	3	3

Japanese Food

Answers on page 243

WELL DONE SO FAR!

Now each player must add up their individual scores from each round to get their total score. The highest score possible is 38. Only the top three scorers can play the final round.

**If you scored
0-20**

So you think you're the *Brainiest*? Hmmm, maybe a little revision wouldn't go amiss. Better luck in the next game!

**If you scored
21–30**

Not bad, not bad at all...but you will have to do better than that to be the *Brainiest*!

**If you scored
31 +**

Wow! Top of the class. May see you in the final round!

Now for the ultimate challenge for the top three scorers. Turn to page 185 and find out if you really are the *Brainiest* of them all!

GAME 6

1

Who was the first host of
the quiz show 'Blockbusters'?

| Les Dennis | 1 | 2 | Max Bygraves |
| Bob Holness | 3 | 4 | Tom O'Connor |

2

Which town was the starting point for a 1936
march to Westminster by unemployed workers?

| Minehead | 1 | 2 | Jarrow |
| Cleethorpes | 3 | 4 | Lowestoft |

3

In Enid Blyton's stories how are Julian, Dick,
Anne, George and Timmy collectively known?

| The Famous Five | 1 | 2 | The Hardy Boys |
| The Perishers | 3 | 4 | The Red Hand Gang |

4

What do MPs in the House of
Commons refer to as 'another place'?

| Buckingham Palace | 1 | 2 | House of Lords |
| Scotland Yard | 3 | 4 | Wales |

Answers on page 234

5

Bob Fosse is a renowned figure in which field of the arts?

Pottery	1	2	Painting
Architecture	3	4	Choreography

6

What is the state capital of Tasmania?

Canberra	1	2	Hobart
Wagga Wagga	3	4	Cairns

7

In which 1984 film do Bill Murray, Dan Aykroyd and Harold Ramis try to save New York from spooks?

Halloween	1	2	Ghostbusters
Creepshow	3	4	Salem's Lot

8

Who said, in 1969, 'No woman in my time will be Prime Minister...'?

Ann Widdecombe	1	2	Betty Boothroyd
Glenys Kinnock	3	4	Margaret Thatcher

Answers on page 234

9

Tim Rice and Elton John's song 'Can You Feel The Love Tonight' features in which film?

A Bug's Life	1	2	The Lion King
Toy Story	3	4	Monsters, Inc.

10

Which country's team won the gold medal in the baseball competition at the 2000 Olympics?

Cuba	1	2	USA
Japan	3	4	South Korea

11

What is yeast a type of?

Enzyme	1	2	Fungus
Animal	3	4	Virus

12

Complete the title of this ghost story by Henry James, 'The Turn of the...'?

Screw	1	2	Lock
Dial	3	4	Wheel

Answers on page 234

Telephone _____ Vault

Town _____ Forward

Lap _____ Hat

Stamp _____ Track

Answers on page 235

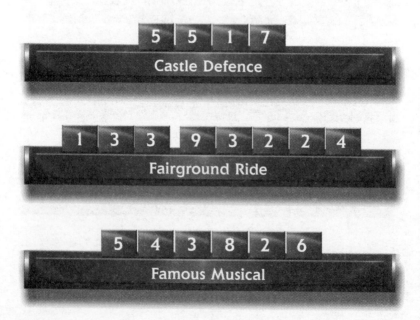

5	5	1	7

Castle Defence

1	3	3	9	3	2	2	4

Fairground Ride

5	4	3	8	2	6

Famous Musical

Answers on page 236

SELECT A CATEGORY

Geography
(page 126)

Sport
(page 128)

Film
(page 130)

The Arts
(page 132)

Music
(page 134)

Natural World
(page 136)

GAME 6

GEOGRAPHY

1

The Ramblas are a series of connected boulevards in which city?

2

The 400 mile long Nelson River flows through which country?

3

What is the official language of Brazil?

4

The Po is the longest river in which country?

5

Which is the world's largest inland sea?

6

What name is given to the line of latitude at 66 degrees 30 minutes north?

Answers on page 239

GEOGRAPHY

7

Cross Fell is the highest point in which British range of hills?

8

Which capital city stands at the confluence of the Parana River and the Rio de la Plata?

9

A tongue of ice that descends from above the snowline, and is constantly replenished from its source, is known as what?

10

Which Italian city is served by Linate airport?

11

The River Trent flows out to the sea via which estuary?

12

What name is given to the lowest level of the Earth's atmosphere?

Answers on page 239

GAME 6

SPORT

1

What was the nationality of former Formula 1 motor racing world champion Ayrton Senna?

2

In which sport is the Stanley Cup contested between clubs from the USA and Canada?

3

Once married to Marilyn Monroe, in which sport was Joe DiMaggio a legendary player?

4

Which English footballer was the inaugural winner of the European Footballer of the Year Award in 1956?

5

In which event did Britain's Mary Rand win a gold medal and set a world record in the 1964 Olympics?

6

Which famous footballer was born Edson Arantes do Nascimento?

Answers on page 239

SPORT

7

In which athletics event did Britain's Roger Black win a silver medal at the 1996 Olympic Games?

8

Which African country's team won the football gold medal at the 1996 Olympic Games?

9

What nationality is the 10,000 metres World and Olympic gold medalist Haile Gebrselassie?

10

Which cyclist won the Tour de France five consecutive times from 1991 to 1995?

11

In 2002, which golfer won the US Masters for the third time?

12

Which football league club is nicknamed the Rams?

Answers on page 240

FILM

1

In which 1986 film does
Jeff Goldblum mutate into an insect?

2

Which 1942 film famously features
the song 'As Time Goes By'?

3

In which Roman Polanski film does Jack
Nicholson play private detective Jake Gittes?

4

The 2001 film 'Iris' was based on the latter
stages of the life of which female author?

5

In which Steven Spielberg film does
Richard Dreyfuss end up in a giant UFO?

6

Which macho actor stars in the
1982 film 'Conan The Barbarian'?

Answers on page 240

FILM

7

Who won an Oscar in 2002 for his role in the cop drama 'Training Day'?

8

Which comedy team stars in the films 'A Day At The Races', 'Duck Soup' and 'Animal Crackers'?

9

Who plays James Bond in the film 'Diamonds Are Forever'?

10

The song 'I've Had The Time Of My Life' comes from which Patrick Swayze movie?

11

What kind of animal is Dumbo?

12

Which was the second 'Star Wars' film to be released?

Answers on page 240

THE ARTS

1

Who painted 'The Laughing Cavalier' in 1624?

2

Which famous ballet company is based
at the Maryinsky Theatre in St Petersburg?

3

What name is given to the form of painting that deals
with optical illusions, as in the work of Bridget Riley?

4

Which art historian presented
the television series 'Civilisation'?

5

What sort of businesses are
Christie's and Sotheby's?

6

Goneril, Cordelia and Regan are the daughters
of which king in a Shakespeare play?

Answers on page 240

THE ARTS

7

Which Russian dancer defected to the West at a Parisian airport in 1961?

8

Who wrote the music for the ballet 'The Rite of Spring'?

9

Which of Shakespeare's works do superstitious actors refer to as 'the Scottish play'?

10

Who would be most likely to use gouache?

11

Which Russian dramatist wrote 'The Seagull' and 'The Cherry Orchard'?

12

The artist Paul Klee described his drawing technique as 'Taking a ... for a walk'?

Answers on page 240

GAME 6

MUSIC

1

Whose third symphony is commonly referred to as the 'Eroica'?

2

Jarvis Cocker is the lead singer of which group?

3

Which opera cycle includes the works 'The Rhinegold', 'The Valkyrie' and 'The Twilight of the Gods'?

4

The instruction 'adagio' indicates that a piece should be played at what tempo?

5

The American song 'My Country 'Tis of Thee' is sung to the same tune as which British anthem?

6

Which British composer wrote the opera 'Gloriana' for the coronation of Queen Elizabeth II?

Answers on page 240

MUSIC

7

Heather Small is the lead singer of which group?

8

Who composed the music for
the ballet 'Nutcracker'?

9

Built in 1776, La Scala is an
opera house in which Italian city?

10

The name of which stringed instrument
is taken from the Hawaiian for 'flea'?

11

Which Italian tenor opened eighteen seasons at New York's
Metropolitan Opera, from its opening night in 1903?

12

In musical notation what is
the term for a half-note?

Answers on page 240

NATURAL WORLD

1

Brent, barnacle and Canada
are species of which sort of bird?

2

Loggerhead and hawksbill are
species of which sort of sea creature?

3

What name is given to the
mouthpart of an insect?

4

Members of which order of fish use a sometimes
luminous lure attached to their snouts to attract prey?

5

Which otter-like creature has become established in
Britain in recent decades after escaping from fur farms?

6

What Japanese name is given to the cultivation of
artificially dwarfed, ornamental trees and shrubs?

Answers on page 240

NATURAL WORLD

7

Which is Britain's only venomous snake?

8

What term is used to describe plants
which live for longer than two years?

9

Which is the largest living land mammal?

10

What are the minute grains, produced by the
structures on the end of stamens in plants, called?

11

Which of the world's oceans is the deepest?

12

What colour are the lobsters
found off the coast of Britain?

Answers on page 240

Interest _____ Sheet

Foreign _____ Card

Banana _____ Cream

Note _____ Plate

Answers on page 242

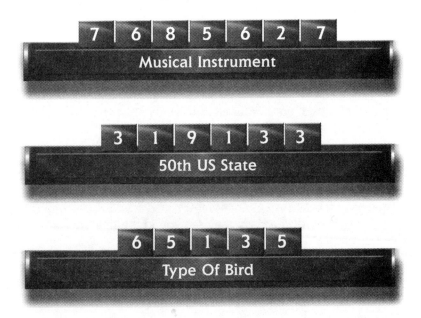

7	6	8	5	6	2	7

Musical Instrument

3	1	9	1	3	3

50th US State

6	5	1	3	5

Type Of Bird

Answers on page 243

WELL DONE SO FAR!

Now each player must add up their individual scores from
each round to get their total score. The highest score possible
is 38. Only the top three scorers can play the final round.

If you scored
0-20

So you think you're the *Brainiest*? Hmmm, maybe a little
revision wouldn't go amiss. Better luck in the next game!

If you scored
21–30

Not bad, not bad at all...but you will have to do
better than that to be the *Brainiest*!

If you scored
31 +

Wow! Top of the class. May see you in the final round!

Now for the ultimate challenge for the top three scorers.
Turn to page 185 and find out if you really are
the *Brainiest* of them all!

GAME 7

1

Augusto Pinochet was dictator of which country?

Cuba	1	2	Mexico
Argentina	3	4	Chile

2

Who co-founded the Democratic
Unionist Party in 1971?

James Callaghan	1	2	Ian Paisley
Gerry Adams	3	4	Edward Heath

3

Which drink was invented by US
pharmacist John S Pemberton in 1886?

Blackcurrant cordial	1	2	Tizer
Coca-Cola	3	4	Lucozade

4

Darjeeling, Assam, and Nilgris
are teas from which country?

India	1	2	China
Sri Lanka	3	4	Philippines

Answers on page 234

5

Which monarch was killed at the Battle of Bosworth Field?

Charles I	1	2	Richard III
George VI	3	4	Henry VIII

6

In which film does George Peppard star alongside Audrey Hepburn?

Breakfast at Tiffany's	1	2	Roman Holiday
My Fair Lady	3	4	The Blue Max

7

Who wrote the poem 'Gunga Din'?

Charles Dickens	1	2	Rudyard Kipling
H G Wells	3	4	George Orwell

8

In 1965 Britain abolished the death penalty for all crimes except what?

Trespassing in Parliament	1	2	Arson
Theft on the railway	3	4	Treason

Answers on page 234

9

According to his 1963 hit, how many 'Hours from Tulsa' was Gene Pitney?

Ten	1	2	Seventy-two
Twenty-four	3	4	Two

10

What nationality was the composer Aaron Copland?

German	1	2	American
British	3	4	French

11

A gourmand is someone who...?

Eats only bread	1	2	Eats too little
Eats too much	3	4	Eats no vegetables

12

What are the out-of-sight areas at the sides of a stage called?

Flies	1	2	Wings
Gods	3	4	Stalls

Answers on page 234

Black _____ Dip

Trigger _____ Birthday

Quiz _____ Off

Power _____ Teacher

Answers on page 235

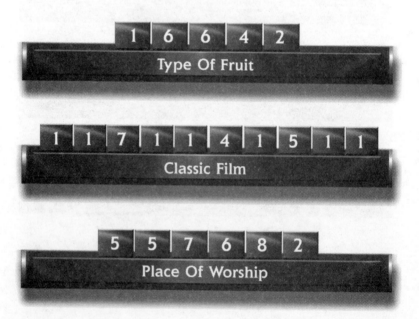

| 1 | 6 | 6 | 4 | 2 |

Type Of Fruit

| 1 | 1 | 7 | 1 | 1 | 4 | 1 | 5 | 1 | 1 |

Classic Film

| 5 | 5 | 7 | 6 | 8 | 2 |

Place Of Worship

Answers on page 236

SELECT A CATEGORY

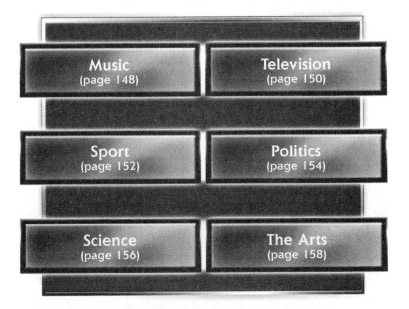

Music
(page 148)

Television
(page 150)

Sport
(page 152)

Politics
(page 154)

Science
(page 156)

The Arts
(page 158)

GAME 7

MUSIC

1

Which pop superstar changed
his name to a symbol in 1993?

2

What two-word musical term, that literally means 'from the head',
instructs a player to repeat from the beginning until the end?

3

Which veteran band was the
first to perform at Live Aid?

4

How many planets feature in
Holst's 'The Planets' suite?

5

Which Oscar-winning actor sings with
a band called 30 Odd Foot of Grunts?

6

Which singer and star of films such as 'The Pajama Game'
and 'Calamity Jane', was born Doris Von Kappelhoff?

Answers on page 240

MUSIC

7

Who composed the music for 'On the Town', 'West Side Story' and the film 'On The Waterfront'?

8

What did Adam and the Ants ask us to 'Stand and' do in their 1981 No 1 single?

9

Niccolò Paganini was a virtuoso famed primarily for his playing of which instrument?

10

The name of which major record label is derived from the surnames of its founders - Herb Alpert and Jerry Moss?

11

How many strings are there on a balalaika?

12

Because of its speed and brevity how is Chopin's famous Waltz in D flat of 1847 commonly known?

Answers on page 240

TELEVISION

1

What is the first name of Sharon and Tracey's next door neighbour in 'Birds of a Feather'?

2

How many lines make up a television picture in the PAL system used in the UK?

3

Tony Randall and Jack Klugman appear together as Felix and Oscar in which US sitcom?

4

What is the name of the department store in 'Are You Being Served?'?

5

Which ill-fated 1990s soap featured nasty Marcus Tandy and roly-poly Bunny Charlson?

6

In which TV sci-fi series does the crew of The Liberator battle The Federation?

Answers on page 240

TELEVISION

7

Which game show has been hosted by Terry Wogan, Les Dawson and Lily Savage?

8

What is the name of Frank Spencer's wife in 'Some Mothers Do 'Ave 'Em'?

9

Windsor Davies and Don Estelle were in the army in which classic sitcom?

10

Which Australian soap reached its 3,000th episode on 22nd February 2002?

11

In 'EastEnders' who is revealed to be Zoe Slater's mother?

12

In 'Tweenies' what sort of creatures are Doodles and Izzles?

Answers on page 240

GAME 7

SPORT

1

> What is the nationality of Formula 1 racing driver Jacques Villeneuve?

2

> Which team played West Ham United in the first FA Cup Final at Wembley, remembered as the 'White Horse' final?

3

> In which event did Britain's Mary Peters win a gold medal at the 1972 Olympics?

4

> Who was awarded the 100 metres gold medal after Ben Johnson was disqualified in the 1988 Olympics?

5

> In which sport did Chris Boardman win a gold medal for Great Britain at the 1992 Olympic Games?

6

> Which British athlete was controversially disqualified from the 1996 Olympic 100m final after two false starts?

Answers on page 240

SPORT

7

Who won the 2002 London Marathon
women's event in record time?

8

Which football club did Terry Venables manage
to the Spanish Championship in 1984?

9

In April 2002, which footballer became the
youngest England captain since Bobby Moore?

10

For which team did George Best
play international football?

11

Which country will host the 2004
European Football Championships?

12

What is the nickname of American
basketball star Earvin Johnson?

Answers on page 240

GAME 7

POLITICS

1

Which country's presidents have included a Valéry, a Charles, a François and a Jacques?

2

What cabinet post was held by Norman Lamont from 1990-1993?

3

Which electoral system is often abbreviated as PR?

4

Which Soviet ruler attended the Yalta conference of 1945?

5

During which decade was James Callaghan prime minister?

6

'Papa Doc' and 'Baby Doc' Duvalier were presidents of which Caribbean state?

Answers on page 240

POLITICS

7

David Ben-Gurion was the first
prime minister of which country?

8

Whom did Tony Blair appoint as
his deputy prime minister in 1997?

9

In which year did the two revolutions take place,
which brought the Bolsheviks to power in Russia?

10

Who was elected First Minister of the
Northern Ireland Assembly in 1998?

11

Which country was taken over by
General Pervez Musharraf in a 1999 coup?

12

Which house in Downing Street has a
letterbox inscribed 'First Lord of the Treasury'?

Answers on page 240

SCIENCE

1

What name is given to the obscuring of light from one celestial body by another?

2

The Archer is an alternative name for which constellation?

3

What is alopecia?

4

Which planet is often called the 'evening star' when visible in the West after sunset?

5

Marsh gas is a common name for which gas?

6

Which Scottish inventor and engineer is primarily associated with a type of road surface?

Answers on page 240

SCIENCE

7

What sort of pen, which revolutionized writing, was patented by Lewis E Waterman in 1884?

8

Which prolific American inventor patented the incandescent light bulb in 1879?

9

Gingivitis is inflammation of what part of the body?

10

Which gas is the main constituent of the sun?

11

What name is given to a group of stars forming a recognisable pattern in the night sky?

12

Which Austrian monk is considered to be the father of genetics?

Answers on page 240

THE ARTS

1

What nationality is the dancer
and choreographer Merce Cunningham?

2

Which forest features in
Shakespeare's 'As You Like It'?

3

Rudolph von Laban invented
a system for the notation of what?

4

Which legendary British ballerina was born
Peggy Hookham in Reigate in 1919?

5

In George Bernard Shaw's play 'Major Barbara',
in which army is the title character a major?

6

Which play opened at the Ambassadors Theatre in London
in 1952, and was still playing at St Martin's Theatre in 2002?

Answers on page 240

THE ARTS

7

What is the musical term for a song sung without instrumental accompaniment?

8

Which four-letter word is the name of an anarchic art movement associated with Marcel Duchamp and Man Ray?

9

Cecil Beaton, Diane Arbus and Bill Brandt are major names in which field of the arts?

10

Which London landmark, completed in 1860, was designed by Sir Charles Barry in the Gothic Revival style?

11

Opened in 1977, which Parisian cultural centre was deisgned by Richard Rodgers and Renzo Piano?

12

Which Belgian Surrealist's paintings are full of optical illusions using men in bowler hats, apples, rocks and windows?

Answers on page 240

Road _____ Party

Video _____ Measure

Steam _____ Sweep

Room _____ Lift

Answers on page 242

8	8	4	7	8	6	2

Bird Of Prey

7	6	8	3	2

Type Of Seafood

1	3	4	4	3	5	3	7	3	1	7	2

London Market

Answers on page 243

WELL DONE SO FAR!

Now each player must add up their individual scores from
each round to get their total score. The highest score possible
is 38. Only the top three scorers can play the final round.

So you think you're the *Brainiest*? Hmmm, maybe a little
revision wouldn't go amiss. Better luck in the next game!

**If you scored
21–30**

Not bad, not bad at all...but you will have to do
better than that to be the *Brainiest*!

**If you scored
31 +**

Wow! Top of the class. May see you in the final round!

Now for the ultimate challenge for the top three scorers.
Turn to page 185 and find out if you really are
the *Brainiest* of them all!

GAME 8

GAME 8

1

In which Spanish city is there an architecturally striking branch of the Guggenheim Museum?

Malaga	1	2	Bilbao
Granada	3	4	Córdoba

2

What is the first name of the character played by Joan Collins in 'Dynasty'?

Alexis	1	2	Krystle
Amanda	3	4	Fallon

3

Which element has the chemical symbol C?

Calcium	1	2	Carbon
Chlorine	3	4	Chromium

4

Who starred in Dennis Potter's TV series 'The Singing Detective'?

Albert Finney	1	2	David Hemmings
Michael Gambon	3	4	Keith Barron

Answers on page 234

GAME 8

5

What is the name of the bear who guides Mowgli through Disney's 1967 classic 'The Jungle Book'?

Baloo	1	2	Kaa
Dizzy	3	4	Louie

6

Molineux is which football team's home ground?

Everton	1	2	Wolverhampton Wanderers
Bradford City	3	4	Middlesbrough

7

In which consecutive Olympics did Carl Lewis win the gold medal for the 100 metres?

1980 and 1984	1	2	1984 and 1988
1988 and 1992	3	4	1992 and 1996

8

Which plant is commonly known as 'lady's ear drops'?

Lily	1	2	Fuchsia
Snapdragon	3	4	Geranium

Answers on page 234

GAME 8

9

Icthyology is the study of what sort of creatures?

Birds	1	2	Fish
Reptiles	3	4	Mammals

10

What is the offspring of a lion and a tigress called?

Liger	1	2	Tion
Hinny	3	4	Hoopy

11

Which novel by E Annie Proulx was made into a film starring Kevin Spacey in 2001?

Heart Songs	1	2	The Shipping News
Accordion Crimes	3	4	Postcards

12

The pampas is a vast plain spreading across which continent?

Asia	1	2	South America
Australia	3	4	Europe

Answers on page 234

Age _____ Year

Window _____ Belt

Country _____ Soda

Pampas _____ Skirt

Answers on page 235

| 7 | 5 | 8 | 1 | 1 | 5 |

Exotic Bird

| | 1 | 1 | 2 | 7 | 1 |

Famous Award

| 4 | 5 | 5 | 2 | 5 | 5 |

Capital City

Answers on page 236

SELECT A CATEGORY

Film
(page 170)

Geography
(page 172)

Food & Drink
(page 174)

Literature
(page 176)

Natural World
(page 178)

History
(page 180)

FILM

1

Who directed the film 'E.T. The Extra-Terrestrial'?

2

Complete the title of this Mel Brooks spoof western, 'Blazing...'?

3

In 2001, which computer game heroine was played on screen by Angelina Jolie?

4

Which 'Godfather' star plays the psychotic Colonel Kurtz in 'Apocalypse Now'?

5

In the film 'Total Recall', Arnold Schwarzenegger's character goes on a 'virtual vacation' to which planet?

6

Which political scandal was the subject of the film 'All The President's Men'?

Answers on page 241

FILM

7

In which Bond film does
Hugo Drax steal a space shuttle?

8

Complete the title of this 1958 sci-fi howler
by Edward D Wood Jr, 'Plan 9 from...'?

9

In 'The Wizard of Oz', which of Dorothy's
travelling companions is made out of metal?

10

Which 1978 film had the tag line
'You'll believe a man can fly!'?

11

Who directed the films
'Annie Hall' and 'Manhattan'?

12

In which 1966 film does a miniaturised submarine carry
doctors around the blood system of a dying scientist?

Answers on page 241

GAME 8

GEOGRAPHY

1

In which city would you be, if you were standing beneath the Brandenburg Gate?

2

On which continent are the Andes mountains?

3

Which city is the state capital of Florida?

4

Which volcano exploded on 27 August 1883 and was heard 2,200 miles away in Australia?

5

Saskatchewan is a province of which country?

6

The railway tunnel between Liverpool and Birkenhead runs under which river?

Answers on page 241

GEOGRAPHY

7

What is the name of the stretch of water that separates Anglesey from mainland Wales?

8

Which famous dam lies on the Arizona-Nevada border?

9

Phnom Penh is the capital of which country?

10

The Shogun were military governors of which country?

11

Which canal connects the Mediterranean Sea to the Red Sea?

12

Until 1945 Shinto was the official religion of which country?

Answers on page 241

GAME 8

FOOD & DRINK

1

Which word derived from the name of a Greek philosopher has come to mean, in a food and wine context, a person of refined taste?

2

What name is given to a bottle containing water which is forced out through a tube by the pressure of gas?

3

With which European city is 'sachertort' associated?

4

Which spirit is distilled from fermented sugar-cane juice or molasses?

5

Which bird is the main ingredient of squab pie?

6

Gunpowder is a variety of which popular beverage?

Answers on page 241

FOOD & DRINK

7

Which English pickle consists of small florets of cauliflower, sliced gherkins, shallots and other vegetables?

8

What would you be eating if you ordered 'pêches' from a French menu?

9

Which kitchen tool is used to cut pastry into strips or serrated narrow bands?

10

What colour is the sweet spicy pepper known as paprika?

11

Paella is a traditional rice dish originating in which country?

12

What name is given to various dishes typical of the cuisine of the region around Nice?

Answers on page 241

LITERATURE

1

Which first novel by Kingsley Amis published in 1954 won the Somerset Maugham prize for fiction?

2

Whose writings transport the reader to 'Rabbit' Angstrom's suburbia and the imaginary state of Kush?

3

Which novel by Wilkie Collins is considered to be the very first detective book in English literature?

4

In the fairy tale, what grew from Jack's magic beans?

5

Which was the first full-length novel to be published by Charles Dickens?

6

William McGonagall famously wrote a poem about which railway disaster?

Answers on page 241

LITERATURE

7

What was the pen name of the 19th century English novelist Mary Ann or Marian Evans?

8

Which of the Brontë sisters used the pseudonym Currer Bell?

9

Who did the Mad Hatter and the March Hare try to put into the teapot in 'Alice's Adventures in Wonderland'?

10

Which literary form is traditionally made up of fourteen lines?

11

What is the name of the famous family which appear in a series of books by John Galsworthy?

12

Which poet wrote the lines, 'I wandered lonely as a cloud/That floats on high o'er vales and hills'?

Answers on page 241

GAME 8

NATURAL WORLD

1

The Bactrian is one of only
two species of which animal?

2

Which word means 'awake during
the day' when applied to animals?

3

What is the main constituent of
the fertiliser known as guano?

4

The Alsatian breed of dog is also known as what?

5

Which fish has types called albacore,
skipjack and yellowfin?

6

To which division of the animal kingdom
do insects and spiders belong?

Answers on page 241

GAME 8

NATURAL WORLD

7

Where on a horse are its withers?

8

What name is given to a male goose?

9

Oil from the liver of which Atlantic fish is a popular source of vitamins A and D?

10

Which is Britain's most common owl?

11

How many arms does a squid typically have?

12

The plantain is most closely related to which fruit?

Answers on page 241

GAME 8

HISTORY

1

What device was first used in France on 25th April 1792, last used there in 1977, and outlawed altogether in 1981?

2

The Mason-Dixon Line is a traditional division between the North and South of which country?

3

Which official of the Church of England traditionally crowns British monarchs?

4

Boutros Boutros-Ghali is a former Secretary-General of which international organisation?

5

Which king of England ordered the compilation of the Domesday Book?

6

The Black Death was an outbreak of plague in which century?

Answers on page 241

HISTORY

7

What date is inscribed on the tablet held by the Statue of Liberty?

8

The dissolution of the monasteries in 1536 took place during the reign of which English king?

9

What is the literal English translation of the German military tactic known as 'blitzkrieg'?

10

President Roosevelt described the attack on Pearl Harbor on 7th December 1941 as a 'date which will live in...' what?

11

In the D-Day landings of June 1944, what were code-named Utah, Juno, Omaha, Gold and Sword?

12

Which American town is famously the site of witch trials that took place from May to October 1692?

Answers on page 241

Passion _____ Bed

Water _____ Film

Iron _____ Cabinet

Post _____ Block

Answers on page 242

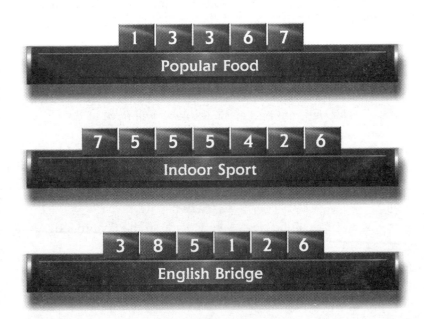

1	3	3	6	7

Popular Food

7	5	5	5	4	2	6

Indoor Sport

3	8	5	1	2	6

English Bridge

Answers on page 243

WELL DONE SO FAR!

Now each player must add up their individual scores from each round to get their total score. The highest score possible is 38. Only the top three scorers can play the final round.

So you think you're the *Brainiest*? Hmmm, maybe a little revision wouldn't go amiss. Better luck in the next game!

Not bad, not bad at all...but you will have to do better than that to be the *Brainiest*!

Wow! Top of the class. May see you in the final round!

Now for the ultimate challenge for the top three scorers. Turn to page 185 and find out if you really are the *Brainiest* of them all!

FINAL ROUND

1ST PLAYER
SELECT YOUR SPECIALIST CATEGORY

1980s	The Simpsons
Fruit & Vegetables	Sea Life
Human Body	Pop Stars
Christmas	Kids TV

Now turn the page to see the pre-picked specialist categories
for the second and third players.

1ST PLAYER SPECIALIST CATEGORY

1980s
(page 189)

2nd player: **Harry Potter** (page 197)
3rd player: **Famous Buildings** (page 205)

The Simpsons
(page 190)

2nd player: **1970s** (page 198)
3rd player: **Famous Criminals** (page 206)

Fruit & Vegetables
(page 191)

2nd player: **Astronomy** (page 199)
3rd player: **US States** (page 207)

Sea Life
(page 192)

2nd player: **1960s** (page 200)
3rd player: **Capital Cities** (page 208)

Human Body
(page 193)

2nd player: **TV Game Shows** (page 201)
3rd player: **Insects** (page 209)

Pop Stars
(page 194)

2nd player: **London Underground** (page 202)
3rd player: **Cartoons** (page 210)

Christmas
(page 195)

2nd player: **TV Sitcoms** (page 203)
3rd player: **1990s** (page 211)

Kids TV
(page 196)

2nd player: **Mammals** (page 204)
3rd player: **Blockbuster Movies** (page 212)

General Knowledge questions start on page 213

1ST PLAYER SPECIALIST CATEGORY:
1980s

1

Which game, invented by a Hungarian professor, was Britain's Toy of the Year in 1980?

2

In which year did the so-called 'Big Bang' revolutionise London's Stock Exchange?

3

In which country did the French secret service sink the Greenpeace ship *Rainbow Warrior* in 1985?

4

Whom did Mikhail Gorbachev succeed as leader of the USSR in 1985?

5

Which country invaded Lebanon in March 1982?

Answers on page 244

1ST PLAYER SPECIALIST CATEGORY:
THE SIMPSONS

1

Who is Marge Simpson's favourite singer?

2

Where does Homer Simpson work?

3

Whom does Bart Simpson idolise?

4

Who created the 'The Simpsons'?

5

What are the names of
Marge Simpson's two sisters?

Answers on page 244

1ST PLAYER SPECIALIST CATEGORY:
FRUIT & VEGETABLES

1

Named after its American creator, which fruit is a cross between a raspberry and a blackberry?

2

What name is given to the edible seeds of leguminous plants such as chickpeas and lentils?

3

How is the Chinese gooseberry more commonly known in the UK?

4

Rocket is cultivated for use as what sort of food?

5

A tangelo is a hybrid of the tangerine and which other fruit?

Answers on page 244

ALL GAMES

1ST PLAYER SPECIALIST CATEGORY:
SEA LIFE

1

Which Asian river's dolphin population
is unique in being blind?

2

Beluga is an alternative name
for which species of whale?

3

Which Antarctic creature is
the largest of the penguin family?

4

By what name is the palm-tree
climbing robber crab also known?

5

By what alternative name are
Norwegian lobsters known?

Answers on page 244

1ST PLAYER SPECIALIST CATEGORY:
HUMAN BODY

1

What is the anatomical name for the collar bone?

2

Where in the body are the metatarsal bones?

3

The olfactory organs handle which of the senses?

4

The bicuspid and tricuspid valves form
part of which organ of the human body?

5

Where in the body are the
gluteus maximus muscles?

Answers on page 244

1ST PLAYER SPECIALIST CATEGORY:
POP STARS

1

Phil Oakley is the lead singer of which
chart-topping electro-pop group?

2

Who sang the theme
song to the film 'Footloose'?

3

Which pop superstar was
born Gordon Matthew Sumner?

4

Which group featured the sneering vocals of
Sean Ryder and the insane dancing of Bez?

5

Who was the lead singer
of Miami Sound Machine?

Answers on page 244

1ST PLAYER SPECIALIST CATEGORY:
CHRISTMAS

1

Which four-week period in the Christian calendar begins on the Sunday closest to St Andrew's Day?

2

What four-letter word is the collective name for the three Wise Men?

3

According to the traditional song, what gift was given for the first time on 'the eighth day of Christmas'?

4

Which yuletide song from the 1942 film 'Holiday Inn' won Irving Berlin an Oscar?

5

In the book by Dr Seuss, which animal 'Stole Christmas'?

Answers on page 244

1ST PLAYER SPECIALIST CATEGORY:
KIDS TV

1

What is the name of the tall blond leader
of the group in 'Scooby Doo, Where Are You?'

2

Who drives around Greendale
with his cat in his van?

3

The Phantom Flan Flinger was a regular mystery
nuisance on which kids' TV show of the 1970s?

4

Which children's news show
celebrated its 30th anniversary in 2002?

5

Which animated gang of toddlers comprises Tommy,
Angelica, Chuckie and the twins Phil and Lil?

Answers on page 244

2ND PLAYER SPECIALIST CATEGORY:
HARRY POTTER

1

For which newspaper does the gossip columnist Rita Skeeter work in 'Harry Potter and The Goblet of Fire'?

2

What are the first names of Harry Potter's friends, the Weasley twins?

3

In 'The Goblet of Fire', what does the elf Dobby tell Harry to eat in order to complete the second task in the Tri-Wizard Tournament?

4

In the Harry Potter books what name is given to non-magical people?

5

In which school house was Harry Potter placed by the Sorting Hat?

Answers on page 245

2ND PLAYER SPECIALIST CATEGORY:
1970s

1

Which term was used by the Khmer Rouge to denote the start of their four-year rule in Cambodia in 1975?

2

Which ready-assembled home computer did Steve Jobs and Steve Wozniak launch in 1977?

3

Which Russian gymnast scored the first ever perfect 10 at the Olympics of 1976?

4

Who was awarded the Nobel Peace Prize in 1979 for her work in India?

5

Which pope died at the age of eighty in 1978?

Answers on page 245

2ND PLAYER SPECIALIST CATEGORY: ASTRONOMY

1

After which astronomer was the giant telescope, launched in the shuttle Discovery in 1990, named?

2

How many sisters make up the cluster of young stars known as the Pleiades?

3

How are the southern lights otherwise known?

4

Which planet lies between Venus and Mars?

5

Which star is known as the North Star or Pole Star?

Answers on page 245

2ND PLAYER SPECIALIST CATEGORY:
1960s

1

Which popular toy, aimed at boys, was launched in the UK by Hasbro in 1964?

2

The prime minister of which country drowned while swimming in December 1967?

3

In which year did the Monterey Pop Festival in San Francisco mark the beginning of the so-called 'Summer of Love'?

4

In 1960, US pilot Gary Powers was shot down while flying his U-2 spy-plane over which country?

5

On which lake was Donald Campbell killed while attempting to break the world water speed record?

Answers on page 245

2ND PLAYER SPECIALIST CATEGORY:
TV GAME SHOWS

1

Which long-running weekday quiz show
is hosted by William G Stewart?

2

Who succeeded Bruce Forsyth
as host of 'The Generation Game'?

3

Which game show's European finals
were called 'Jeux Sans Frontières'?

4

Which TV talent contest featured
Hughie Greene and his 'clapometer'?

5

Emlyn Hughes and Bill Beaumont were long-
running team captains on which quiz show?

Answers on page 245

2ND PLAYER SPECIALIST CATEGORY:
LONDON UNDERGROUND

1

On the London Underground map
what colour is the District Line?

2

Which London Underground line runs from
West Ruislip in the west to Epping in the east?

3

On which London Undergound line is Brixton?

4

Which airport is directly connected to the
London Underground with two stations?

5

Which London Underground line, originally
known as the Fleet Line, was renamed in 1977?

Answers on page 245

2ND PLAYER SPECIALIST CATEGORY:
TV SITCOMS

1

What is the name of Rik Mayall's
character in 'The New Statesman'?

2

Eddie, Lily, Grandpa, Marilyn and Herman
make up which classic TV sitcom family?

3

What colour were the coats worn by the
entertainers at Maplin's Holiday Camp in 'Hi-de-Hi!'?

4

Which ex-Goon wrote and
appeared in 'Potty Time'?

5

Which of the 'Two Ronnies'
starred in the sitcom 'Sorry'?

Answers on page 245

ALL GAMES

2ND PLAYER SPECIALIST CATEGORY:
MAMMALS

1

A leveret is a young what?

2

The okapi is native to which continent?

3

Which creature did the Romans
refer to as the 'spotted camel'?

4

How many digits do pigs' hooves have each?

5

What is the name of the greasy substance found
in wool that is extracted and used in ointments?

Answers on page 245

3RD PLAYER SPECIALIST CATEGORY:
FAMOUS BUILDINGS

1

Which property mogul sold the Empire State Building for $57.5 million in 2002?

2

In the Vatican Palace what is the name of the Pope's private chapel?

3

Which famous Moorish palace and fortress overlooks the city of Granada in Spain?

4

Which king of England ordered the construction of the Tower of London?

5

What stands at the centre of the Place Charles de Gaulle in Paris?

Answers on page 246

3RD PLAYER SPECIALIST CATEGORY:
FAMOUS CRIMINALS

1

John George Haigh used which ingenious method to dispose of his victim's bodies?

2

Whom did Robert Ford shoot in the back in 1882?

3

Mr and Master Robinson were the aliases of which famous murderer and his lover?

4

Which infamous couple lived at 25 Cromwell Street, Gloucester?

5

In which country did Ronnie Biggs, the Great Train Robber, spend much of the last thirty years?

Answers on page 246

3RD PLAYER SPECIALIST CATEGORY:
US STATES

1

Which US State's motto is
'Mountaineers are always free'?

2

Which was the first US State to
be admitted to the Union in 1787?

3

According to a 2000 census,
which is the most populous US State?

4

The capital of which US State shares its name
with a Native American tribe of the Great Plains?

5

Which southern US State is
known as the 'Heart of Dixie'?

Answers on page 246

3RD PLAYER SPECIALIST CATEGORY:
CAPITAL CITIES

1

Which is the northernmost national
capital city in the world?

2

What was the former capital of Australia?

3

In which capital city is the famous Trevi Fountain?

4

Which capital city lies on the
River Baradá in south-west Syria?

5

Washington DC is bounded
on one side by which river?

Answers on page 246

3RD PLAYER SPECIALIST CATEGORY:
INSECTS

1

Adult insects' bodies are divided into three sections: the head, the abdomen, and which other?

2

How many pairs of legs do insects have?

3

What is the common name for the crane fly?

4

What is the name of the substance fed to young bees by workers to turn them into queens?

5

What is the name of the red dye obtained from the crushed, dried bodies of the insect Dactylopius coccus?

Answers on page 246

ALL GAMES

3RD PLAYER SPECIALIST CATEGORY:
CARTOONS

1

In which park does Yogi Bear live?

2

Which canine cartoon lawman is harassed by Muskie the Muskrat?

3

Who does Adam, Prince of Eternia become when he holds aloft his mighty sword?

4

Which bionic Interpol officer is aided by his clever niece Penny and a dog called Brain?

5

What kind of animal is Quick Draw McGraw?

Answers on page 246

3RD PLAYER SPECIALIST CATEGORY:
1990s

1

Which UK government scheme, launched in 1991, aimed to improve standards of public service?

2

Who was Wimbledon men's singles champion seven times during the 1990s?

3

Which newspaper magnate disappeared from his yacht and died under mysterious circumstances in 1991?

4

Which former American football star was arrested after a slow-moving car chase and tried in 1995 for the murder of his ex-wife?

5

What Latin phrase did the Queen use to describe the troubled year 1992?

Answers on page 246

3RD PLAYER SPECIALIST CATEGORY:
BLOCKBUSTER MOVIES

1

Who stars as lawyer-on-the-run Bobby Dean in the 1998 conspiracy thriller 'Enemy of the State'?

2

In which 1999 film does Brad Pitt organise underground bare knuckle boxing matches?

3

Which Italian comedian directs and stars in the 1997 Oscar-winning film 'Life is Beautiful'?

4

Who co-stars as a Hollywood actress alongside Hugh Grant in 'Notting Hill'?

5

Which child actor stars in both 'The Sixth Sense' and 'AI: Artificial Intelligence'?

Answers on page 246

GENERAL KNOWLEDGE

1

How many parts does a tetralogy have?

2

In which Middle East country
is the historic city of Petra?

3

Which Hindu god is often represented
as having the head of an elephant?

4

Formerly known as Hellespont, which strait
links the Aegean Sea with the Sea of Marmara?

5

With which animal is the French region
called the Camargue particularly associated?

6

Which 19th century US novelist and humorist is quoted as
saying 'reports of my death have been greatly exaggerated'?

Answers on page 247

GENERAL KNOWLEDGE

7

What is the European continental equivalent of a size nine shoe in the UK?

8

Which Greek word for 'retribution' means the inescapable person or thing that will bring about your downfall?

9

During which season of the year are you most likely to experience 'dog days'?

10

What name is given to a financial investor who buys a security in the hope that it will go up?

11

The 19th century Opium Wars took place between Britain and which other nation?

12

In what would a vexillologist be interested?

Answers on page 247

GENERAL KNOWLEDGE

13

Which science deals with the production of very low temperatures and its applications?

14

RAI is the state broadcaster in which European country?

15

In which year did the Maastricht treaty come into effect?

16

In cricket, what name is given to a ball bowled higher than a full toss which endangers the batsman?

17

Which renowned British-born film director is quoted as saying 'There is no terror in a bang, only in the suspense'?

18

Camberwell Beauty is a species of which insect?

Answers on page 247

GENERAL KNOWLEDGE

19

In boxing, with which
hand does a southpaw lead?

20

Which British author wrote 'The Collector', 'The
Magus' and 'The French Lieutenant's Woman'?

21

What name is given to someone
who makes or sells women's hats?

22

By what former name was South Africa's
Free State province known before 1994?

23

From which country did the USA make the
Louisiana Purchase in the 19th century?

24

In which British institution is Black
Rod responsible for keeping order?

Answers on page 247

GENERAL KNOWLEDGE

25

Which primate is sometimes known as 'the wild man of the woods' after its Malay name?

26

What word means both a non-ordained member of a Church and a person without specialised knowledge of a subject?

27

Of what are Sans-serif, Grotesque and Venetian all kinds?

28

How is the South American Rio de la Plata known in English?

29

For what does the 'L' stand in the acronym of the trade union ASLEF?

30

In which country is the headquarters of the European Central Bank?

Answers on page 247

GENERAL KNOWLEDGE

31

Which unit is used to
measure electrical resistance?

32

What name is given to an otter's lair?

33

Which novel by Patricia Highsmith was made
into a film starring Jude Law and Matt Damon?

34

Which Scottish city is served by Dyce airport?

35

The Davis Cup is a major
competition in which sport?

36

Which institution is popularly known
as the 'Old Lady of Threadneedle Street'?

Answers on page 247

GENERAL KNOWLEDGE

37

Which foodstuff was used in the Renaissance painting technique called tempera?

38

The first Nobel Peace Prize was awarded to the leader of which international organisation?

39

Apart from London, in which other city would you find Cleopatra's Needle?

40

Which architectural term is used to describe the front or principal face of a building?

41

In which city is the headquarters of the global news agency Reuters?

42

Which aristocratic Romantic poet did Lady Caroline Lamb describe as 'mad, bad and dangerous to know'?

Answers on page 247

GENERAL KNOWLEDGE

43

What is the name of the U-shaped harp-like instrument that was popular in ancient Greece?

44

Copenhagen's seafront famously features a statue of which fairytale character?

45

Who was the Roman messenger of the gods?

46

Viticulture is the science of cultivating what?

47

Which British national daily newspaper was founded in 1986?

48

What expression, taken from an American gambling term, is used to describe the most highly regarded business shares?

Answers on page 247

GENERAL KNOWLEDGE

49

Over which mountain range does the hot southerly wind called the Föhn blow?

50

Which famous Italian fashion house started life as a saddlery in Florence in 1906?

51

Which creature is the symbol of the World Wide Fund for Nature?

52

What is the English translation of the weather phenomenon called 'El Niño'?

53

Which Saint's day is 1st March?

54

Of which British island group are North and South Uist a part?

Answers on page 247

ALL GAMES

GENERAL KNOWLEDGE

55

For what does the abbreviation
IBM stand in the business world?

56

Which two-word Latin term applies to proceedings
that take place in a judge's private chambers?

57

On which continent are the ruins
of the ancient city of Carthage?

58

Clumber, cocker and springer are
all breeds of which type of dog?

59

What is an inverted V-shaped
pattern on a heraldic shield called?

60

What name is given to the
central calm area of a hurricane?

Answers on page 247

GENERAL KNOWLEDGE

61

Which British city is sometimes referred
to as the 'Athens of the North'?

62

According to Lord Tennyson, how many rode 'into the
valley of death' in 'The Charge of the Light Brigade'?

63

Magistrates of which ancient empire were preceded
by officials carrying bundles of rods called fasces?

64

Which mammal is Britain's largest land carnivore?

65

In which modern country was the kingdom
of Castile founded in the 10th century?

66

Which organisation was superseded
by the United Nations in 1946?

Answers on page 247

GENERAL KNOWLEDGE

67

Brine is water saturated with which substance?

68

Which national daily newspaper reverted to its original name in 2002, and dropped its red banner, calling it 'sleazy'?

69

Of which Greek island group are Andros, Naxos and Paros a part?

70

What nationality was the 15th century explorer known as John Cabot?

71

What name is given to the science which studies the evolution and origin of the universe?

72

Which country left the Commonwealth in 1961 and rejoined in 1994?

Answers on page 247

GENERAL KNOWLEDGE

73

How many American colonies signed the
Declaration of Independence in 1776?

74

Members of which profession are
sometimes referred to as the 'Fourth Estate'?

75

To which sea does the Manchester
Ship Canal link the city?

76

What is meant by the musical
instruction 'allegro'?

77

Which artificial language was
constructed in 1887 by L L Zamenhof?

78

In which city are the headquarters
of the European Space Agency?

Answers on page 247

GENERAL KNOWLEDGE

79

Which chess term is used to describe an opening move in which a piece is sacrificed to secure an advantageous position?

80

What part of a church is its campanile?

81

Which country was renamed the Democratic Republic of Congo in 1997?

82

In Roman mythology, of what was Pluto the god?

83

To what did Karl Marx refer as being 'the opium of the people'?

84

Often used by medieval artists, what name was given to the darkened box with a tiny hole used for projecting an image onto a screen inside?

Answers on page 247

GENERAL KNOWLEDGE

85

In which sport might you come
across a nightwatchman?

86

Which two oceans does the
Strait of Magellan link?

87

In which satirical novel by Jonathan Swift does
the narrator visit the land of Brobdingnag?

88

What is the French word for cake?

89

Mathematically speaking, what name is
given to angles of more than 180 degrees?

90

In music, how many quavers
are there in a crotchet?

Answers on page 247

GENERAL KNOWLEDGE

91

Which group of Caribbean islands is divided between Britain and the USA?

92

In classical mythology, who ferried the dead across the River Styx?

93

In which country was the national newspaper El Pais founded?

94

What name is given to a slender tower attached to a mosque?

95

Which British prime minister was known as the Grand Old Man?

96

In which South American country is the Atacama Desert?

Answers on page 247

GENERAL KNOWLEDGE

97

Who is the only US president to have served more than two terms?

98

Which trade organisation superseded GATT in 1995?

99

What is the former name of Taiwan?

100

Of which national tabloid did Piers Morgan become editor in 1994?

101

What does the abbreviation EP on a record stand for?

102

From which building on the Acropolis were the Elgin Marbles taken?

Answers on page 247

GENERAL KNOWLEDGE

103

What is the name of the brilliant blue mineral used as a pigment by medieval artists?

104

With which two countries does the principality of Andorra share its borders?

105

What was the name of the Jamaican house owned by James Bond creator Ian Fleming?

106

Which word is used in fencing as an acknowledgement of a hit by an opponent?

107

By what name was Belize known until 1973?

108

With which fashion accessories would you associate the designer Philip Treacy?

Answers on page 247

GENERAL KNOWLEDGE

109

In which sport might you use a penholder grip?

110

Which cheese is most likely to be found in a traditional Greek salad?

111

How is the seventh Wednesday before Easter known in the Christian calendar?

112

What number do the Roman numerals XC represent?

113

Which picture succeeded 'The Full Monty' as the highest-grossing British film in 1999?

114

In which Scandinavian country was the composer Edvard Grieg born?

Answers on page 247

GENERAL KNOWLEDGE

115

In which European country would you
find Moorish palaces called alcazars?

116

What is the SI unit called the
hertz used to measure?

117

In Norse mythology, what name is given to the
maidens who took dead heroes to Valhalla?

118

On the third Saturday of which
month is the Queen's official birthday?

119

Which Welsh term, meaning 'sitting', is used to describe a
traditional gathering dedicated to music, poetry and literature?

120

What name is given to a beaver's young?

Answers on page 247

ANSWERS

ROUND 1

GAME 1
1	2	**2**	1	**3**	4	**4**	1	**5**	2	**6**	4	**7** 2
8	3	**9**	2	**10**	2	**11**	1	**12**	2			

GAME 2
1	1	**2**	3	**3**	2	**4**	1	**5**	2	**6**	3	**7** 4
8	2	**9**	4	**10**	4	**11**	3	**12**	2			

GAME 3
1	1	**2**	2	**3**	1	**4**	2	**5**	3	**6**	4	**7** 3
8	2	**9**	1	**10**	2	**11**	1	**12**	2			

GAME 4
1	3	**2**	2	**3**	1	**4**	3	**5**	2	**6**	3	**7** 4
8	2	**9**	1	**10**	4	**11**	1	**12**	2			

GAME 5
1	4	**2**	1	**3**	2	**4**	4	**5**	2	**6**	1	**7** 3
8	2	**9**	3	**10**	1	**11**	3	**12**	2			

GAME 6
1	3	**2**	2	**3**	1	**4**	2	**5**	4	**6**	2	**7** 2
8	4	**9**	2	**10**	1	**11**	2	**12**	1			

GAME 7
1	4	**2**	2	**3**	3	**4**	1	**5**	2	**6**	1	**7** 2
8	4	**9**	3	**10**	2	**11**	3	**12**	2			

GAME 8
1	2	**2**	1	**3**	2	**4**	3	**5**	1	**6**	2	**7** 2
8	2	**9**	2	**10**	1	**11**	2	**12**	2			

MISSING LINKS

GAME 1
Salad; Pot; Cheese; Panel

GAME 2
Office; Fish; House; Boot

GAME 3
Neck; Squash; Card; Fish

GAME 4
Flower; Runner; Case; Car

GAME 5
Cream; Farm; Food; Board

GAME 6
Pole; Centre; Top; Album

GAME 7
Sheep; Happy; Show; Supply

GAME 8
Gap; Seat; Club; Grass

CODEBREAKERS

GAME 1
Big Ben; Ton; Bali

GAME 2
Oak; Perm; Trapeze

GAME 3
Heart; Cucumber; Picasso

GAME 4
Poppy; Leg; Golf

GAME 5
Ostrich; Poker; Umbrella

GAME 6
Moat; Big Wheel; Oliver!

GAME 7
Apple; Casablanca; Mosque

GAME 8
Toucan; BAFTA; London

ROUND 2

GAME 1
POLITICS: 1 Boris Yeltsin; 2 Isle of Man; 3 Edinburgh; 4 Two;
5 Hirohito; 6 Republic of Ireland; 7 Sinn Fein; 8 Six years;
9 Argentina; 10 Lenin; 11 Labour; 12 Fifth Amendment
MUSIC: 1 Bryan Ferry; 2 Trout; 3 REM; 4 Paris; 5 Genesis;
6 Black; 7 The Monkees; 8 Pink Floyd; 9 Sisters; 10 Nothing;
11 The Smiths; 12 Mondays
HISTORY: 1 Red; 2 Prince Harry (Henry); 3 Four score and
seven (87); 4 Robert I (The Bruce); 5 Operation Desert Storm;
6 Rudolf Hess; 7 Thor Heyerdahl; 8 Prince of Wales;
9 Hindenburg; 10 Edward; 11 Soviet Union; 12 France
GEOGRAPHY: 1 Seine; 2 South Africa; 3 Himalayas; 4 Nomad;
5 La Guardia; 6 Mount St. Helens; 7 Cancer; 8 Mount Elbrus; 9
Cornwall; 10 Art museum; 11 The Alps; 12 Tokyo
FOOD & DRINK: 1 Swiftlet/swift; 2 Garlic; 3 Cellar; 4 Dundee
cake; 5 Schnapps; 6 Baguette; 7 Mace; 8 Frankfurter;
9 Self-raising; 10 Brut; 11 Raisins; 12 Mushroom
FILM: 1 Marilyn Monroe; 2 Saving Private Ryan; 3 Mel Gibson;
4 Jaws; 5 Damien; 6 Jackie Chan; 7 The Great Escape; 8 Errol
Flynn; 9 Aliens; 10 Fantasia; 11 Spock; 12 Britney Spears

GAME 2
LITERATURE: 1 Lord Peter Wimsey; 2 Dopey; 3 Rudyard Kipling;
4 Pathos; 5 Robert Burns; 6 Kenneth Graham; 7 Pushmi-pullyu;
8 Iceland; 9 Monkey; 10 Tom Sharpe; 11 Brideshead; 12 Muse
NATURAL WORLD: 1 4; 2 Venus flytrap; 3 Robin; 4 New
Zealand; 5 Dog (Terrier); 6 Stamen; 7 Krill; 8 Mountain ash;
9 Puffin; 10 Busy Lizzy; 11 Puffer fish; 12 Dock
SCIENCE: 1 Nicolaus Copernicus; 2 Tears; 3 Pantyhose/Tights;
4 640; 5 Aorta; 6 Chiropody; 7 Mercury; 8 Eye; 9 Sax;
10 Nine; 11 Saliva; 12 Electric battery
TELEVISION: 1 Sun Hill; 2 Grange Hill; 3 Steve Coogan;
4 Sarah-Jane; 5 Brian Cant; 6 The Prisoner; 7 Take The High
Road; 8 Witch; 9 Billy Connolly; 10 Talk shows; 11 Pikachu;
12 Tony Robinson
THE ARTS: 1 Halle Berry; 2 Salvador Dali; 3 Death of a
Salesman; 4 The Mona Lisa; 5 Kitsch; 6 The Rockettes;
7 Othello; 8 Jackson Pollock; 9 Michael Flatley;

10 Ballet Rambert (Rambert Dance Company); **11** A leg;
12 Nutcracker
SPORT: 1 Salt Lake City; **2** Flo-Jo; **3** Commonwealth Games;
4 Derek Redmond; **5** Shooting; **6** London Marathon; **7** Heats
were on a Sunday; **8** Cycling; **9** Churchill Downs; **10** Preston
North End; **11** Polo; **12** Marathon

GAME 3

TELEVISION: 1 Wilfred Brambell; **2** Lisa Riley; **3** Martians;
4 Wish You Were Here...?; **5** The Tweenies; **6** Prisoner: Cell
Block H; **7** Edmund; **8** Soo; **9** Patrick Mower; **10** Spain;
11 Torchy; **12** Spike Milligan
HISTORY: 1 North Vietnam; **2** Defender of the Faith; **3** Hong
Kong; **4** York; **5** Hydrogen bomb; **6** Balaclava; **7** Denmark;
8 Bangladesh; **9** Prince Philip; **10** Nikita Khrushchev;
11 *Lusitania*; **12** American Civil War
THE ARTS: 1 Brown; **2** Cubism; **3** Roof; **4** The Royal Ballet;
5 Henri de Toulouse-Lautrec; **6** Dress rehearsal; **7** Pre-
Raphaelites; **8** Overacting; **9** Andy Warhol; **10** Fred Astaire;
11 Richard III; **12** Clarice Cliff
MUSIC: 1 Finnish; **2** Andrew Lloyd-Webber; **3** Massachusetts;
4 Two; **5** Handel; **6** Wine; **7** Cats; **8** Wilfred Owen; **9** Flowers;
10 Nutbush; **11** Violin; **12** Pink Panther
GEOGRAPHY: 1 Apartheid; **2** Ethiopia; **3** The Southern Cross;
4 Declaration of Independence; **5** Sri Lanka; **6** Liffey; **7** Mecca;
8 ETA; **9** Klondike; **10** Peru; **11** Rhine; **12** Sitting Bull
POLITICS: 1 Italy; **2** Conservative Party; **3** Karl Marx; **4** China;
5 Homosexuality; **6** Al Gore; **7** George Washington; **8** Anwar
Sadat; **9** Robin Day; **10** Ronald Reagan; **11** Militant Tendency;
12 House of Representatives

GAME 4

FOOD & DRINK: 1 Eve's; **2** Switzerland; **3** Eggs; **4** Choux;
5 Easter; **6** Dumplings; **7** (Scottish) Cheese; **8** Plums; **9** Neck;
10 Eggs; **11** Dripping; **12** Okra
SCIENCE: 1 Barium; **2** Bubble gum; **3** Hamstrings; **4** Box
camera; **5** Pituitary; **6** Jacques Cousteau; **7** Charles II; **8** Cell;
9 Big-bang theory; **10** Waxing; **11** Pluto; **12** Samuel Colt
NATURAL WORLD: 1 Greenpeace; **2** Lizard; **3** Red deer;
4 Bat; **5** Antennae; **6** Pear; **7** Basking shark; **8** Melon; **9** Fox;

10 Calf; 11 Wasps; 12 Seaweed
FILM: 1 Dinosaurs; 2 A donkey; 3 Gandalf; 4 Batman;
5 Flubber; 6 Airplane!; 7 Big; 8 David Lynch; 9 Kevin Costner;
10 Braveheart; 11 Soylent Green; 12 Kwai
SPORT: 1 Arsenal; 2 Ski jump; 3 St Leger; 4 Durham; 5 Charlton;
6 Jonathan Edwards; 7 Moffitt; 8 Australia; 9 Andre Agassi; 10
Chris Chataway; 11 West Ham United; 12 Show jumping
LITERATURE: 1 John; 2 The Legend of Sleepy Hollow; 3 Ray
Bradbury; 4 Feet; 5 Ghost writer; 6 Albatross; 7 The Spy;
8 Raven; 9 Miss Bianca; 10 W H Auden; 11 Andrew Motion;
12 H G Wells

GAME 5
HISTORY: 1 Ireland; 2 Gallipoli; 3 Harold II; 4 Bay of Pigs;
5 Vietnam War; 6 Ethelred; 7 Iraq; 8 Windsor; 9 Erwin
Rommel; 10 Wessex; 11 Princess Royal; 12 Knights
LITERATURE: 1 The African Queen; 2 E H Shepard; 3 13¾;
4 The Wonderful Wizard of Oz; 5 Sir Walter Scott; 6 Wild Swans;
7 Wessex; 8 Alexander Solzhenitsyn; 9 The Fat Controller; 10 The
Satanic Verses; 11 Charlie and the Chocolate Factory; 12 T S Eliot
SCIENCE: 1 X-rays; 2 Vinegar; 3 Desmond Morris; 4 Zenith;
5 Carburettor; 6 The Rocket; 7 Hydrogen; 8 Femur; 9 Dr
Christiaan Barnard; 10 Hippocrates; 11 German; 12 Plane tree
FOOD & DRINK: 1 Pine resin; 2 Risotto; 3 Colour; 4 Tea;
5 Zest; 6 Tutti-frutti; 7 Calf's head; 8 Sec; 9 Yeast; 10 Tokay;
11 Tapas; 12 Plums
POLITICS: 1 John Major; 2 Triangular; 3 Helmut; 4 Michael
Heseltine; 5 Nelson Mandela; 6 Kyoto; 7 Yugoslavia;
8 Richard Nixon; 9 Margaret Thatcher; 10 Democratic Party;
11 Norma; 12 Red Crescent
TELEVISION: 1 Teenage Mutant Hero Turtles; 2 Dr Matt
Ramsden; 3 Bart Simpson; 4 Annie Walker; 5 David Dimbleby;
6 Wellard; 7 Brookside; 8 Compo; 9 High definition; 10 Bud
Flanagan; 11 Stomach; 12 Allo 'Allo!

GAME 6
GEOGRAPHY: 1 Barcelona; 2 Canada; 3 Portuguese; 4 Italy;
5 Caspian Sea; 6 Arctic Circle; 7 Pennines; 8 Buenos Aires;
9 Glacier; 10 Milan; 11 Humber estuary; 12 Troposphere
SPORT: 1 Brazilian ; 2 Ice hockey; 3 Baseball; 4 Stanley

Matthews; **5** Long jump; **6** Pelé; **7** 400 metres; **8** Nigeria;
9 Ethiopian; **10** Miguel Induráin; **11** Tiger Woods; **12** Derby
County

FILM: 1 The Fly; **2** Casablanca; **3** Chinatown; **4** Iris Murdoch;
5 Close Encounters of the Third Kind; **6** Arnold Schwarzenegger;
7 Denzel Washington; **8** The Marx Brothers; **9** Sean Connery;
10 Dirty Dancing; **11** An elephant; **12** The Empire Strikes Back

THE ARTS: 1 Frans Hals; **2** Kirov Ballet; **3** Op art; **4** Kenneth
Clark; **5** Auction houses; **6** King Lear; **7** Rudolf Nureyev; **8** Igor
Stravinsky; **9** Macbeth; **10** An artist; **11** Anton Chekhov; **12** Line

MUSIC: 1 Beethoven; **2** Pulp; **3** The Ring of the Nibelung;
4 Slow; **5** God Save The Queen; **6** Benjamin Britten; **7** M People;
8 Tchaikovsky; **9** Milan; **10** Ukulele; **11** Enrico Caruso; **12** Minim

NATURAL WORLD: 1 Goose; **2** Turtle; **3** Mandible; **4** Angler
fish; **5** Mink; **6** Bonsai; **7** Adder; **8** Perennial; **9** (African)
Elephant; **10** Pollen; **11** Pacific; **12** Blue/black

GAME 7

MUSIC: 1 Prince; **2** Da capo; **3** Status Quo; **4** Seven; **5** Russell
Crowe; **6** Doris Day; **7** Leonard Bernstein; **8** Deliver; **9** Violin;
10 A&M; **11** Three; **12** Minute Waltz

TELEVISION: 1 Dorien; **2** 625; **3** The Odd Couple; **4** Grace
Brothers; **5** Eldorado; **6** Blake's 7; **7** Blankety Blank; **8** Betty;
9 It Ain't Half Hot Mum; **10** Home and Away; **11** Kat (Slater);
12 Dogs

SPORT: 1 Canadian; **2** Bolton Wanderers; **3** Pentathlon;
4 Carl Lewis; **5** Cycling; **6** Linford Christie; **7** Paula Radcliffe;
8 Barcelona; **9** Michael Owen; **10** Northern Ireland;
11 Portugal; **12** Magic

POLITICS: 1 France; **2** Chancellor of the Exchequer; **3**
Proportional representation; **4** Joseph Stalin; **5** 1970s; **6** Haiti;
7 Israel; **8** John Prescott; **9** 1917; **10** David Trimble; **11**
Pakistan; **12** Number 10

SCIENCE: 1 Eclipse; **2** Sagittarius; **3** Hair loss; **4** Venus;
5 Methane; **6** John McAdam; **7** Fountain pen; **8** Thomas
Edison; **9** Gums; **10** Hydrogen; **11** Constellation; **12** Mendel

THE ARTS: 1 American; **2** Forest of Arden; **3** Dance steps;
4 Dame Margot Fonteyn; **5** Salvation Army; **6** The Mousetrap;
7 A capella; **8** Dada; **9** Photography; **10** Houses of Parliament;
11 The Pompidou Centre; **12** René Magritte

GAME 8

FILM: 1 Steven Spielberg; 2 Saddles; 3 Lara Croft; 4 Marlon Brando; 5 Mars; 6 Watergate; 7.Moonraker; 8 Outer Space; 9 The Tin Man; 10 Superman; 11 Woody Allen; 12 Fantastic Voyage

GEOGRAPHY: 1 Berlin; 2 South America; 3 Tallahassee; 4 Krakatoa; 5 Canada; 6 Mersey; 7 Menai Strait; 8 Hoover Dam; 9 Cambodia; 10 Japan; 11 Suez Canal; 12 Japan

FOOD & DRINK: 1 Epicure; 2 Siphon; 3 Vienna; 4 Rum; 5 Pigeon; 6 Tea; 7 Piccalilli; 8 Peaches; 9 Pastry wheel; 10 Red; 11 Spain; 12 Niçoise

LITERATURE: 1 Lucky Jim; 2 John Updike; 3 The Moonstone; 4 Giant beanstalk; 5 Oliver Twist; 6 The Tay Bridge Disaster; 7 George Eliot; 8 Charlotte; 9 The Dormouse; 10 Sonnet; 11 The Forsyte family; 12 William Wordsworth

NATURAL WORLD: 1 Camel; 2 Diurnal; 3 Bird droppings; 4 German shepherd; 5 Tuna; 6 Arthropoda; 7 Shoulders; 8 Gander; 9 Cod; 10 Tawny owl; 11 Ten; 12 Banana

HISTORY: 1 The guillotine; 2 USA; 3 Archbishop of Canterbury; 4 United Nations; 5 William I (The Conqueror); 6 14th; 7 July 4, 1776; 8 Henry VIII; 9 Lightning war; 10 Infamy; 11 (Landing) Beaches; 12 Salem

MISSING LINKS

GAME 1
Light; Line; Clip; Skate

GAME 2
Watch; Table; Proof; Roller

GAME 3
Diving; Light; Egg; Piece

GAME 4
Trainer; Screen; Pin; Cut

GAME 5
Cookie; Box; Cutting; Trap

GAME 6
Charge; Travel; Skin; Paper

GAME 7
Works; Tape; Clean; Service

GAME 8
Flower; Feature; Filing; Office

CODEBREAKERS

GAME 1
Everest; Pig; Spatula

GAME 2
Custard; Mole; Cheshire

GAME 3
Barley; Football; Potato

GAME 4
Samosa; Tea; Arsenal

GAME 5
Beef; Pier; Sushi

GAME 6
Trumpet; Hawaii; Robin

GAME 7
Vulture; Squid; Billingsgate

GAME 8
Chips; Snooker; Humber

FINAL ROUND

1ST PLAYER SPECIALIST CATEGORIES

1980s: 1 Rubik's Cube; 2 1986; 3 New Zealand; 4 Konstantin Chernenko; 5 Israel

THE SIMPSONS: 1 Tom Jones; 2 Springfield Nuclear Power Plant; 3 Krusty the Clown; 4 Matt Groening; 5 Patty and Selma

FRUIT & VEGETABLES: 1 Loganberry; 2 Pulses; 3 Kiwi fruit; 4 Salad plant; 5 Grapefruit

SEA LIFE: 1 Ganges; 2 White whale; 3 Emperor penguin; 4 Coconut crab; 5 Dublin Bay prawns

HUMAN BODY: 1 Clavicle; 2 In the foot; 3 Smell; 4 Heart; 5 In the buttocks

POP STARS: 1 The Human League; 2 Kenny Loggins; 3 Sting; 4 Happy Mondays; 5 Gloria Estefan

CHRISTMAS: 1 Advent; 2 Magi; 3 Eight maids-a-milking; 4 White Christmas; 5 The Grinch

KIDS TV: 1 Fred; 2 Postman Pat; 3 Tiswas; 4 Newsround; 5 Rugrats

2ND PLAYER SPECIALIST CATEGORIES

HARRY POTTER: 1 The Daily Prophet; 2 Fred and George;
3 Gillyweed; 4 Muggles; 5 Gryffindor

1970s: 1 Year Zero; 2 Apple II; 3 Nadia Comaneci; 4 Mother Teresa; 5 Pope Paul VI

ASTRONOMY: 1 Hubble; 2 Seven; 3 Aurora australis; 4 Earth;
5 Polaris

1960s: 1 Action Man; 2 Australia; 3 1967; 4 USSR; 5 Coniston Water

TV GAME SHOWS: 1 Fifteen To One; 2 Larry Grayson; 3 It's a Knockout; 4 Opportunity Knocks!; 5 A Question of Sport

LONDON UNDERGROUND: 1 Green; 2 Central Line; 3 Victoria Line; 4 Heathrow Airport; 5 Jubilee Line

TV SITCOMS: 1 Alan B'Stard; 2 The Munsters; 3 Yellow;
4 Michael Bentine; 5 Ronnie Corbett

MAMMALS: 1 Hare; 2 Africa; 3 Giraffe; 4 Four; 5 Lanolin

3RD PLAYER SPECIALIST CATEGORIES

FAMOUS BUILDINGS: 1 Donald Trump; 2 Sistine Chapel;
3 Alhambra Palace; 4 William I (The Conqueror); 5 Arc De
Triomphe

FAMOUS CRIMINALS: 1 Acid baths; 2 Jesse James; 3 Dr
Crippen; 4 Fred and Rosemary West; 5 Brazil

US STATES: 1 West Virginia; 2 Delaware; 3 California;
4 Wyoming; 5 Alabama

CAPITAL CITIES: 1 Reykjavik; 2 Melbourne; 3 Rome;
4 Damascus; 5 Potomac

INSECTS: 1 Thorax; 2 Three; 3 Daddy long legs; 4 Royal jelly;
5 Cochineal

CARTOONS: 1 Jellystone Park; 2 Deputy Dawg; 3 He-Man;
4 Inspector Gadget; 5 A horse

1990s: 1 Citizen's Charter; 2 Pete Sampras; 3 Robert Maxwell;
4 O J Simpson; 5 Annus horribilis

BLOCKBUSTER MOVIES: 1 Will Smith; 2 Fight Club; 3 Roberto
Benigni; 4 Julia Roberts; 5 Haley Joel Osment

GENERAL KNOWLEDGE

1 Four; 2 Jordan; 3 Ganesh; 4 Dardanelles; 5 Horse;
6 Mark Twain; 7 43; 8 Nemesis; 9 Summer; 10 Bull; 11 China;
12 Flags; 13 Cryogenics; 14 Italy; 15 1993; 16 Beamer;
17 Alfred Hitchcock; 18 Butterfly; 19 Right; 20 John Fowles;
21 Milliner; 22 Orange Free State; 23 France; 24 House of
Lords; 25 Orang-utan; 26 Layman; 27 Typefaces; 28 River
Plate; 29 Locomotive; 30 Germany; 31 Ohm; 32 Holt;
33 The Talented Mr Ripley; 34 Aberdeen; 35 Tennis; 36 Bank
of England; 37 Egg (yolk); 38 Red Cross; 39 New York;
40 Facade; 41 London; 42 Lord Byron; 43 Lyre; 44 The Little
Mermaid; 45 Mercury; 46 Grapes; 47 The Independent;
48 Blue chip; 49 Alps; 50 Gucci; 51 Panda; 52 The Child;
53 St David; 54 Outer Hebrides; 55 International Business
Machines; 56 In camera; 57 Africa; 58 Spaniel; 59 Chevron;
60 Eye; 61 Edinburgh; 62 Six hundred; 63 Roman; 64 Badger;
65 Spain; 66 League of Nations; 67 Common salt; 68 Daily
Mirror; 69 Cyclades; 70 Italian; 71 Cosmology; 72 South
Africa; 73 Thirteen; 74 Press; 75 Irish Sea; 76 Quickly;
77 Esperanto; 78 Paris; 79 Gambit; 80 Bell-tower; 81 Zaïre;
82 Underworld; 83 Religion; 84 Camera obscura; 85 Cricket;
86 Pacific and Atlantic; 87 Gulliver's Travels; 88 Gateau;
89 Reflex; 90 Two; 91 Virgin Islands; 92 Charon; 93 Spain;
94 Minaret; 95 Gladstone; 96 Chile; 97 Franklin D Roosevelt;
98 WTO (World Trade Organisation); 99 Formosa; 100 News
of the World; 101 Extended-play; 102 Parthenon; 103 Lapis
lazuli; 104 France and Spain; 105 Goldeneye; 106 Touché;
107 British Honduras; 108 Hats; 109 Table tennis; 110 Feta;
111 Ash Wednesday; 112 90; 113 Notting Hill; 114 Norway;
115 Spain; 116 Frequency; 117 Valkyries; 118 June;
119 Eisteddfod; 120 Kittens

SCORE SHEETS

NAME

ROUND 1

1	2	3	4	5	6	7	8	9	10	11	12

MISSING LINKS

1	
2	
3	
4	

CODE BREAKERS

1	
2	
3	

ROUND 2

1	2	3	4	5	6	7	8	9	10	11	12

MISSING LINKS

1	
2	
3	
4	

CODE BREAKERS

1	
2	
3	

FINAL ROUND

PLAYER 1					PLAYER 2					PLAYER 3				
1	2	3	4	5	1	2	3	4	5	1	2	3	4	5

WINNER

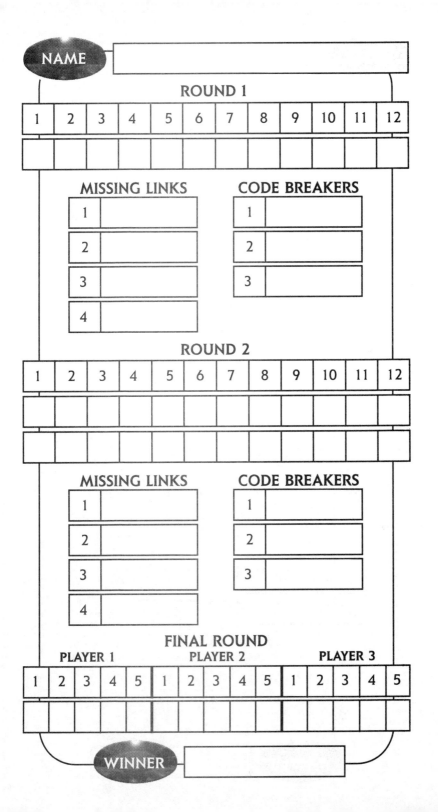

NAME

ROUND 1

1	2	3	4	5	6	7	8	9	10	11	12

MISSING LINKS

1	
2	
3	
4	

CODE BREAKERS

1	
2	
3	

ROUND 2

1	2	3	4	5	6	7	8	9	10	11	12

MISSING LINKS

1	
2	
3	
4	

CODE BREAKERS

1	
2	
3	

FINAL ROUND

PLAYER 1					PLAYER 2					PLAYER 3				
1	2	3	4	5	1	2	3	4	5	1	2	3	4	5

WINNER

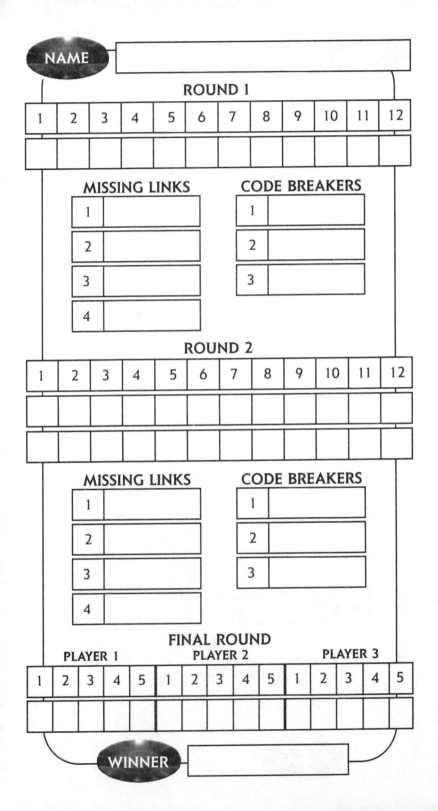

NAME

ROUND 1

1	2	3	4	5	6	7	8	9	10	11	12

MISSING LINKS

1	
2	
3	
4	

CODE BREAKERS

1	
2	
3	

ROUND 2

1	2	3	4	5	6	7	8	9	10	11	12

MISSING LINKS

1	
2	
3	
4	

CODE BREAKERS

1	
2	
3	

FINAL ROUND

PLAYER 1					PLAYER 2					PLAYER 3				
1	2	3	4	5	1	2	3	4	5	1	2	3	4	5

WINNER

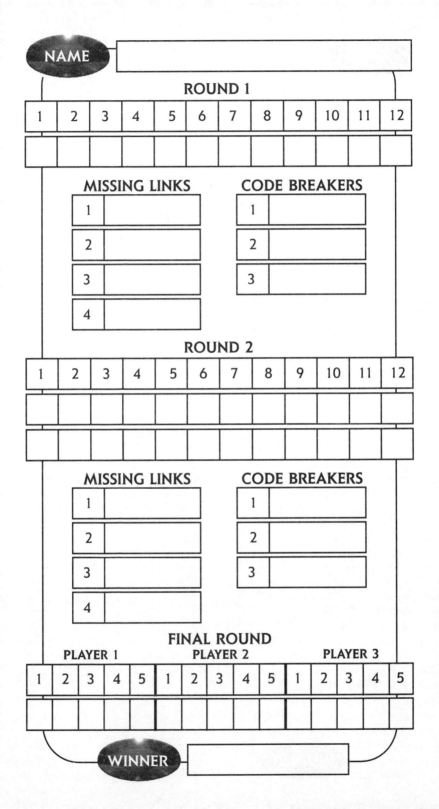

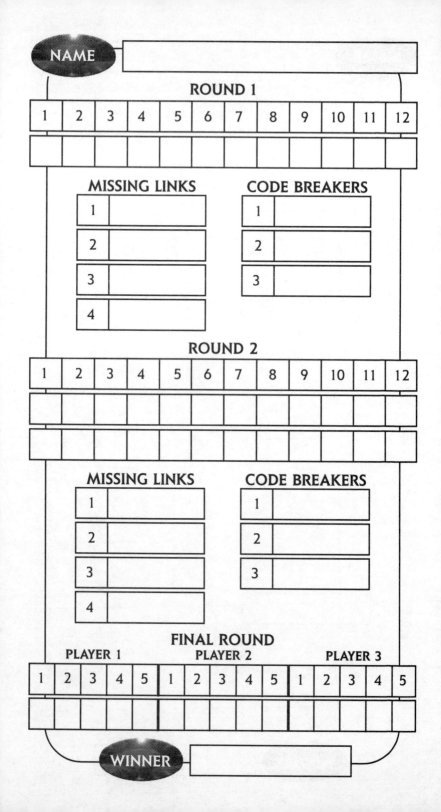

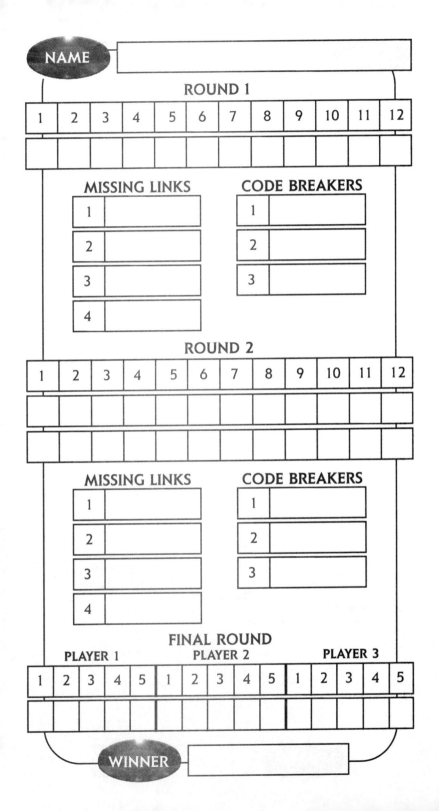

NAME

ROUND 1

1	2	3	4	5	6	7	8	9	10	11	12

MISSING LINKS

1	
2	
3	
4	

CODE BREAKERS

1	
2	
3	

ROUND 2

1	2	3	4	5	6	7	8	9	10	11	12

MISSING LINKS

1	
2	
3	
4	

CODE BREAKERS

1	
2	
3	

FINAL ROUND

PLAYER 1					PLAYER 2					PLAYER 3				
1	2	3	4	5	1	2	3	4	5	1	2	3	4	5

WINNER

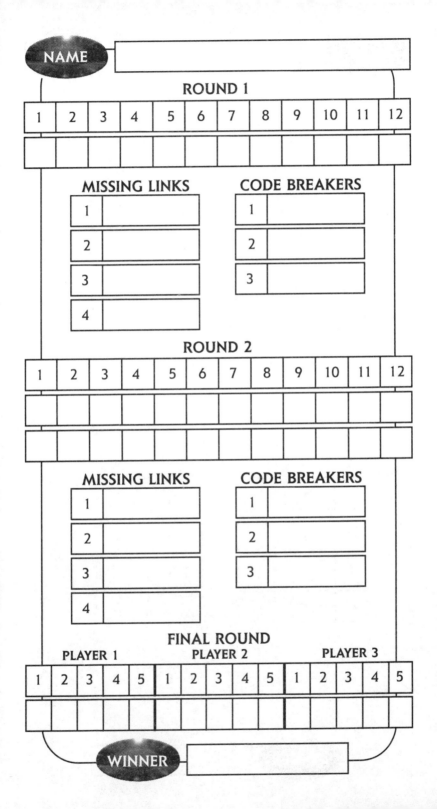

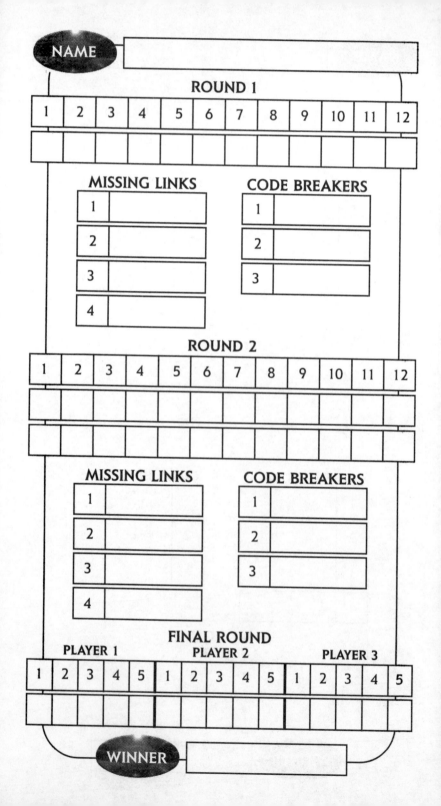

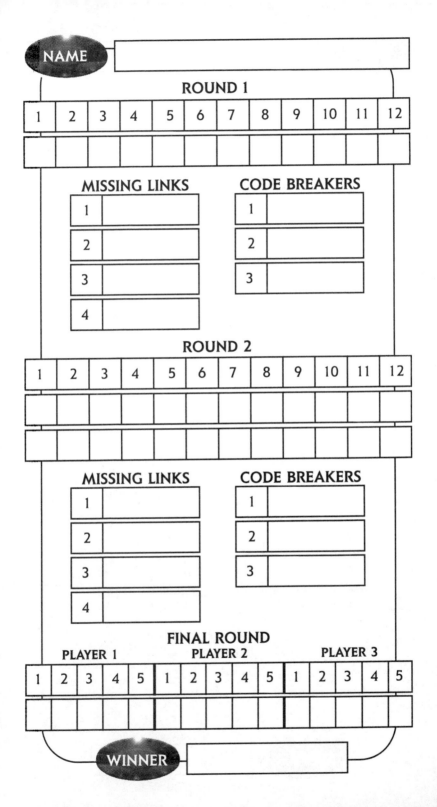

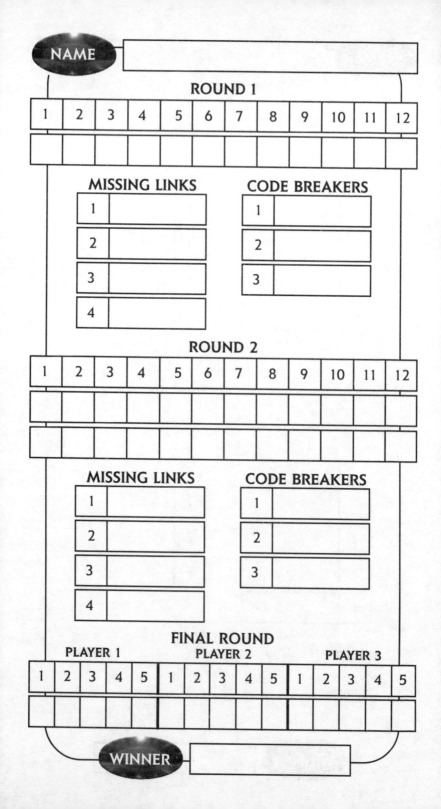

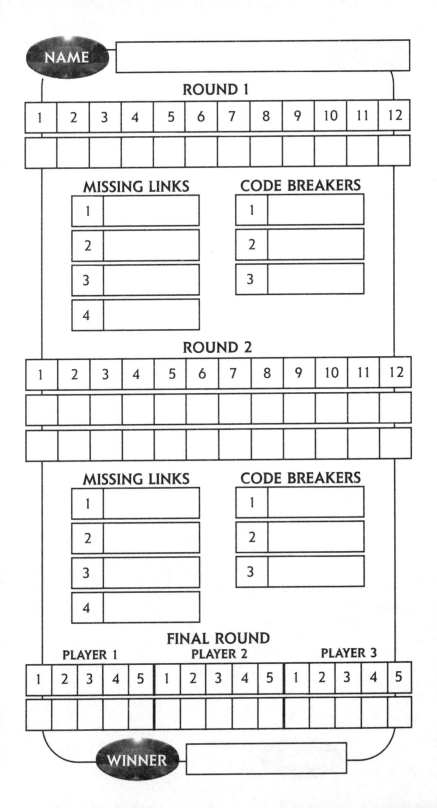

NAME

ROUND 1

1	2	3	4	5	6	7	8	9	10	11	12

MISSING LINKS

1	
2	
3	
4	

CODE BREAKERS

1	
2	
3	

ROUND 2

1	2	3	4	5	6	7	8	9	10	11	12

MISSING LINKS

1	
2	
3	
4	

CODE BREAKERS

1	
2	
3	

FINAL ROUND

PLAYER 1					PLAYER 2					PLAYER 3				
1	2	3	4	5	1	2	3	4	5	1	2	3	4	5

WINNER

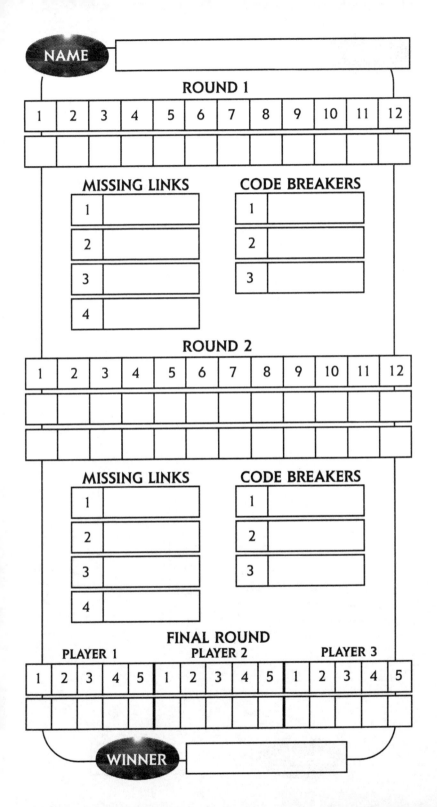

NAME

ROUND 1

1	2	3	4	5	6	7	8	9	10	11	12

MISSING LINKS

1	
2	
3	
4	

CODE BREAKERS

1	
2	
3	

ROUND 2

1	2	3	4	5	6	7	8	9	10	11	12

MISSING LINKS

1	
2	
3	
4	

CODE BREAKERS

1	
2	
3	

FINAL ROUND

PLAYER 1					PLAYER 2					PLAYER 3				
1	2	3	4	5	1	2	3	4	5	1	2	3	4	5

WINNER

NAME

ROUND 1

1	2	3	4	5	6	7	8	9	10	11	12

MISSING LINKS

1	
2	
3	
4	

CODE BREAKERS

1	
2	
3	

ROUND 2

1	2	3	4	5	6	7	8	9	10	11	12

MISSING LINKS

1	
2	
3	
4	

CODE BREAKERS

1	
2	
3	

FINAL ROUND

PLAYER 1					PLAYER 2					PLAYER 3				
1	2	3	4	5	1	2	3	4	5	1	2	3	4	5

WINNER

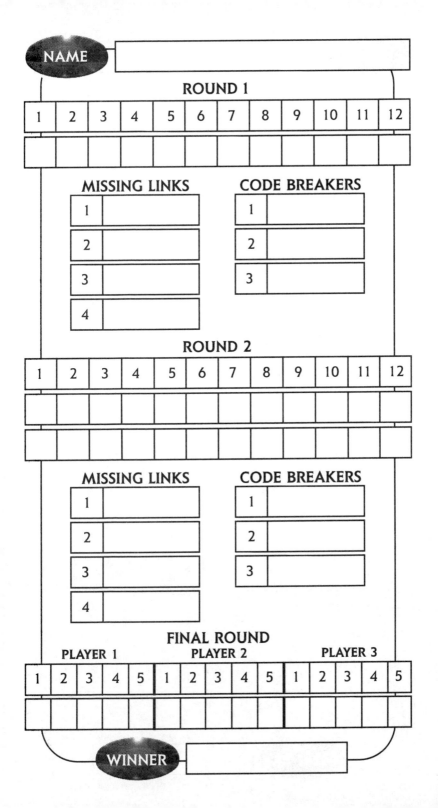

NAME

ROUND 1

1	2	3	4	5	6	7	8	9	10	11	12

MISSING LINKS

1	
2	
3	
4	

CODE BREAKERS

1	
2	
3	

ROUND 2

1	2	3	4	5	6	7	8	9	10	11	12

MISSING LINKS

1	
2	
3	
4	

CODE BREAKERS

1	
2	
3	

FINAL ROUND

PLAYER 1					PLAYER 2					PLAYER 3				
1	2	3	4	5	1	2	3	4	5	1	2	3	4	5

WINNER

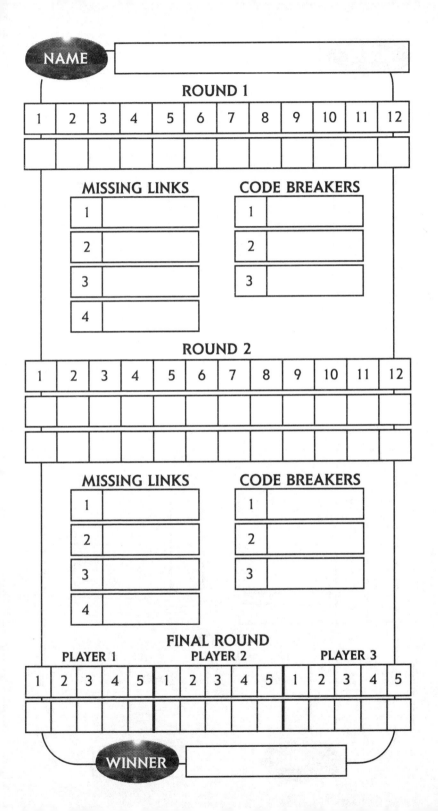

NAME

ROUND 1

1	2	3	4	5	6	7	8	9	10	11	12

MISSING LINKS

1	
2	
3	
4	

CODE BREAKERS

1	
2	
3	

ROUND 2

1	2	3	4	5	6	7	8	9	10	11	12

MISSING LINKS

1	
2	
3	
4	

CODE BREAKERS

1	
2	
3	

FINAL ROUND

PLAYER 1					PLAYER 2					PLAYER 3				
1	2	3	4	5	1	2	3	4	5	1	2	3	4	5

WINNER

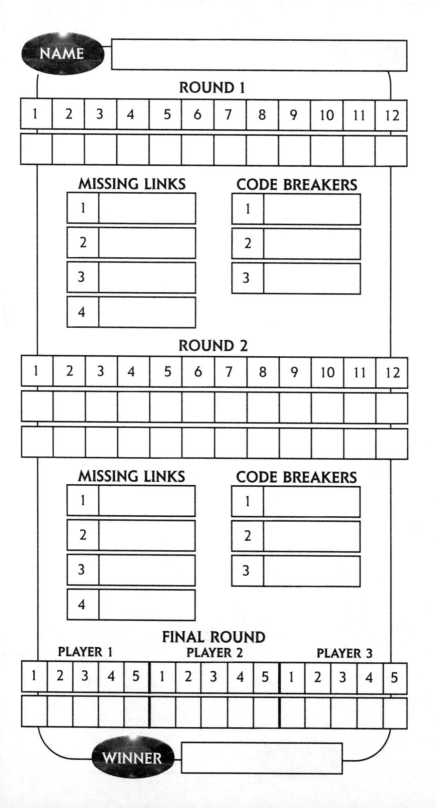

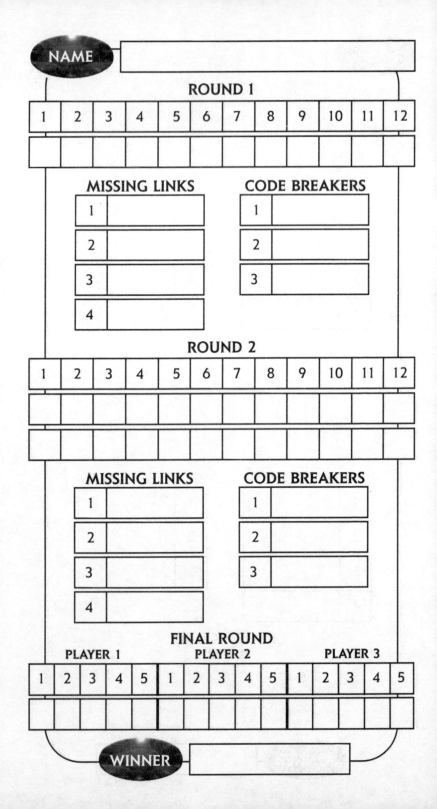